Our Freedom
in Christ

Books in this series . . .

A BIBLE STUDY ON ROMANS

Our Freedom in Christ

REUBEN R. WELCH

FRANCIS ASBURY PRESS
of Zondervan Publishing House
Grand Rapids, Michigan

OUR FREEDOM IN CHRIST:
A Bible Study on Romans
Copyright © 1988 by Reuben R. Welch

FRANCIS ASBURY PRESS is an imprint of Zondervan Publishing House
1415 Lake Drive, S.E., Grand Rapids, Michigan 49506

Library of Congress Cataloging in Publication Data

Welch, Reuben R.
    Our freedom in Christ : a Bible study on Romans / Reuben R. Welch.
        p.   cm.
    ISBN 0-310-75251-5
    1. Bible. N.T. Romans—Criticism, interpretation, etc. I. Title.
BS2665.2.W44   1988
227'.106—dc19   87-34909
                                                                      CIP

Unless otherwise noted, all Scripture texts are quoted from the Revised Standard Version of the Bible, copyright © 1946, 1952, 1971, 1973 by the Division of Christian Education, National Council of the Churches of Christ in the United States of America, and are used by permission.

Scripture quotations marked NIV are taken from the *Holy Bible: New International Version* (North American Edition), copyright © 1973, 1978, 1984, by the International Bible Society. Used by permission of Zondervan Bible Publishers.

Scripture quotations marked PHILLIPS are taken from *The New Testament in Modern English,* revised edition, copyright © 1958, 1960, 1972 by J. B. Phillips. Scripture quotations marked KJV are taken from the *King James Version.*

Edited by Joseph D. Allison
Designed by Ann Cherryman

Printed in the United States of America

88 89 90 91 92 93 94 95 / CH / 10 9 8 7 6 5 4 3 2 1

CONTENTS

Preface

● Romans is the longest, the most theological, and by far the most influential of Paul's letters. It has been like dynamite in the life of the Christian church. Augustine, hungry for God but bound by his lusts, found light and freedom through the reading of Romans 13:13–14: "Not in reveling and drunkenness, not in debauchery and licentiousness, not in quarreling and jealousy, but put on the Lord Jesus Christ, and make no provision for the flesh, to gratify its desires."

Luther's hungry heart despaired of ever being worthy of the fearful, righteous God. Through the study and teaching of Romans he came to understand the "righteousness of God" and "that righteousness whereby, through grace and sheer mercy, he justifies by faith." That discovery was to him like a "gateway to heaven."

It was while listening to someone read from Luther's preface to the Book of Romans that John Wesley, who all his life had struggled and failed to find peace with God, felt his own heart "strangely warmed" and was enabled to trust Christ for his salvation, receiving an assurance that his sins were taken away.

No one can measure the influence of these men. And how many others of us have had our lives transformed by the power of the Spirit at work through this book? It is not an easy book to study, but it has a way of getting inside us as we get into it—and we can never be the same.

Paul was in Corinth when he wrote it, A.D. 56 or 57. He was on his way to Jerusalem with the offerings he had been collecting to help "the poor among the saints" there (15:26). That done, he intended to go on to Spain by way of Rome (15:28).

Romans is different because Paul wrote it to a church he had not established, a church he had never even visited. It was a mix of Jews and Gentiles, some of whom misunderstood or mistrusted the apostle. His teachings would not be accepted easily by the Jews concerned to preserve the law, and there could be opposition. But Paul wanted to know the church and share in its life. He was eager to declare to them the gospel for which he had been "set apart," and he needed their good will and support for his mission to Spain. So he wrote a letter of introduction to prepare the way for his coming.

Though not as personal as Paul's other writings, Romans has special value for us because it presents in an orderly way some of the greatest and most precious truths of the gospel. All through Romans I have found the great theme of freedom. In Christ there is freedom from guilt, from alienation, from our own selves, from the law, and from the power of sin and death. More than that, we have freedom, through the Spirit of Christ, to live in hope and joy through the weaknesses and the sufferings of this present life. Giving our whole selves to him, we are free to participate, as members of his church, in his saving purposes for the Jews, for ourselves, and for our whole wide world.

It is my hope that these theme studies in Romans will help us open our hearts to the wonderful grace gift of our freedom in Christ.

CHAPTER · 1

What Is
the Gospel?

Paul, a servant of Jesus Christ, called to be an apostle, set apart for
the gospel of God which he promised beforehand through his
prophets in the holy scriptures, the gospel concerning his Son, who
was descended from David according to the flesh and designated Son
of God in power according to the Spirit of holiness by his
resurrection from the dead, Jesus Christ our Lord, through whom we
have received grace and apostleship to bring about the obedience of
faith for the sake of his name among all the nations, including
yourselves who are called to belong to Jesus Christ;

To all God's beloved in Rome, who are called to be saints:

Grace to you and peace from God our Father and the Lord Jesus
Christ. . . .

I am under obligation both to Greeks and to barbarians, both to the
wise and to the foolish: so I am eager to preach the gospel to you also
who are in Rome.

For I am not ashamed of the gospel; it is the power of God for
salvation to every one who has faith, to the Jew first and also to the
Greek. For in it the righteousness of God is revealed through faith
for faith; as it is written, "He who through faith is righteous shall
live" (Rom. 1:1–7, 14–17).

● Three times in this Scripture passage, Paul uses the word *gospel*
in a significant way: "[I am] set apart for the gospel. . . . I am eager
to preach the gospel. . . . I am not ashamed of the gospel. . . ." The
gospel, he says, "is the power of God for salvation to every one

9

who has faith." That is, the gospel is God's dynamic to save. The saving power of God is released through the gospel message.

But what is the gospel? Whatever it is, when the apostles first preached it, it nearly turned their world upside down—or right side up. What New Testament evangelists proclaimed had a freshness, a life, and a healing power that brought new strength to an old and tired culture. Our own culture, in spite of the marvelous achievements of its incredible technology, is dying for want of a new and saving word of truth and life. That word is *gospel*. It literally means "good news" or "good message." Paul says that it is God's good news; and that, of course, is the whole point. Our own news has been bad news. So what is God's good news? What makes the gospel *gospel* and not just helpful instruction or inspiration?

• A Promising God

The first thing Paul tells us about the gospel is that it was "promised beforehand through his prophets in the holy scriptures" (v. 2). In fact, almost all New Testament preaching begins with this same declaration. Whether to Jews or Gentiles, to religious or nonreligious people, to civilized or barbarian, the word is the same: The promises of God are fulfilled in the coming of Jesus; the new age of God's kingdom has dawned in the Christ event; the old word of promise has found its fulfillment.

On the Day of Pentecost, Peter said, "This is what was spoken by the prophet" (Acts 2:16), and then he quoted Joel 2:28–32. The martyr Stephen in his defense to the Jews rehearsed the long history of Israel and concluded: "Which of the prophets did not your fathers persecute? And they killed those who announced beforehand the coming of the Righteous One, whom you have now betrayed and murdered" (Acts 7:52). On his first missionary journey, in Pisidian Antioch, Paul preached in the synagogue, "God has brought to Israel a Savior, Jesus, as he promised" (Acts 13:23).

Why is this proclamation of the new thing God is doing in Jesus always tied to the promises that were made in the Old Testament? I believe that is an important question.

The tie between God's promises and their fulfillment is in fact central to the very gospel itself. Jesus did not simply appear suddenly on the world scene. His coming was the fulfillment of the age-long purposes of God, which had been declared by his prophets. Study Bibles have their charts of this prophecy; prophecy preachers have their pictures and pamphlets about it; the whole world hears about it at Christmastime. Christmas carolers sing it, the Christmas dramas portray it, and all the pageantry reveals it: Jesus came in fulfillment of prophecy.

But we haven't said enough, because prophecy is not simply the foretelling of future events. Prophets were not strange, holy visionaries who saw unknown things yet to come. It is indeed wonderful that God would reveal the future to his prophets. But we need to see a deeper truth about prophecy. Prophets were not simply predictors. They were keenly aware of what was going on in their society. They were people who had visions of God, who heard words from God about their present situation, who declared to others what God was doing and what he would do in their world and in their unique historical situation.

So when we say that the Christ event is the fulfillment of prophecy, we are saying that God has purposes for every era of human history. We are saying that God makes promises and that he works with men and women to bring his promises to pass. The God who promises is the God who is at work through current events to fulfill what he has promised. That is very good news! God does not promise things and then they coincidentally happen. His prophecies do not merely "come to pass"; they are *brought to pass* by the activity of God, who works through the activities of real men and women in real events. If we say that the gospel is the fulfillment of prophecy, that is another way of saying that God is at work to fulfill his promises on the field of human history.

In the process of accomplishing his goals, God relates to and works with people as they are and where they are. The Creator of our race has involved himself with the history of our race. He enters into relationship with his created people.

From the question in the Garden of Eden ("Where are you?") to the deliverance accomplished through Noah, to the promise given and sustained through Abraham, to the Exodus and the covenant established through Moses at Sinai, through the struggles of the period of the judges, into the era of the monarchy and the new covenant with David, through the loss of the Northern Kingdom to the exile and return of Judah—in judgment and deliverance, through law and prophet, priest and king, God has involved himself savingly with his people. Then, in the fullness of time, he sent his Son, in whom "all the promises of God find their Yes" (2 Cor. 1:20).

Can we see what this means? It means that History is his story too. The eternal, sovereign, Father God has locked himself into the human situation. That puts our human situation in a whole new light, the light of God, who is present with us and who is Lord.

We are saved, then, from emptiness and meaninglessness and hopelessness. We have a Father. Our world is not an orphanage. We are not alone in a galaxy without meaning, living out a history that is going nowhere. God was not at his wits' end when he fashioned this little spinning ball; it has not somehow spun out of his grasp. God is still God. He is in charge, and he is present. And when the last word of this world is said, he will say it.

I read of a dial-a-prayer service for atheists: No one answers. Seriously, I can think of nothing worse than to cry out to God— from the depths of my isolated humanity, from my cosmic loneliness—and get no answer. I cannot imagine how devastating it would be to knock on heaven's door and find no one at home.

Do you suppose that our almost feverish drive to probe space in search of other life forms is motivated by the hidden fear that we are alone in the universe? What if we would finally discover that there is no life anywhere, other than our own? The idea that there are no other beings in the universe is intolerable. That is an awful thought. If all we have is ourselves, if all there is is what we are, then ultimately nothing else really matters. And because so many believe this is true, we can understand the existential despair of our time. That despair cries out for the presence of someone else to give some meaning beyond ourselves, someone to relieve us of the intolerable burden of our cosmic isolation and emptiness.

The good news of the gospel is that we are *not* alone. Someone else is here. The heavenly Father is here, and he has taken the initiative to communicate with us. He has broken into our desperate monologue, has involved himself with us in our human situation, and is working in our history to accomplish his ultimate purposes of grace.

The fulfillment of prophecy that occurred when Christ was born has profound implications for every human being. The apostles knew that Jesus' birth was not an interruption nor an exception to God's eternal plan; it was an intrinsic, climactic part of his saving purpose for all mankind. The coming of the Messiah confirmed God's intimate engagement with our earthly lives. We are not left to create meaning for ourselves.

We Christians are not blind to the presence of evil in our world. We cannot ignore the demonic forces of destruction. We are not deaf to the cries of suffering and tragedy. But all these things reaffirm that the gospel is good news. The gospel tells us that God is not blind to, ignorant of, or deaf to the realities of our human condition. He has made promises to us, and he has worked in our history—worked with us—to bring them to fulfillment. He has purposed good; he will accomplish good. He is in charge, even in the presence of evil. And that is very good news.

● An Incarnate God

The second thing that makes the gospel good news is that it concerns God's Son, "who was descended from David according to the flesh and designated Son of God in power according to the Spirit of holiness by his resurrection from the dead, Jesus Christ our Lord" (1:3–4). The heart of the Christian message is that the Lord of history has entered history in person. The good news is not something, it is *Someone.* Our faith is not in a doctrine, nor in a belief, nor even in the truth—it is in Jesus our Lord, who said, "I am . . . the truth" (John 14:6).

Jesus is fully human. The phrase "descended from David according to the flesh" (v. 3) tells us that Jesus had a family tree; he was born of a long and noble family line. God came into this world to do his work in Jesus, who is as truly human as we are. Jesus is God come all the way to where we are to save us. That is incredibly good news.

God does not do his work from afar. He crosses the distance between himself and us. He enters fully into our situation and takes to himself all that it means to be human. He takes to himself all that our guilt means, all that our emptiness, alienation, and estrangement mean. That is the way the Lord works. He locks himself into our humanity and saves us from "inside" our situation.

A missionary could parachute into a lost tribal community and try to "save" it by breaking down the old ways and replacing them with new and better ones. Or the same missionary could enter into the life of the community in love and care, to teach and to live— perhaps to die—as one at home. To use one of H. H. Farmer's analogies, the loom of tribal life would not be destroyed; rather, a new and different thread would be introduced into the fabric of their lives, a thread that would subtly but inevitably change the pattern. The cloth of their history would continue to come off the same loom, but its design would ultimately be transformed. I believe this is the way Jesus comes into our history. He becomes a part of our human community, introducing a new and transform-ing thread into the fabric of our history.

Jesus enters the arena of our sin and sorrow and need, going to the depths of our fallenness. Remember the words of the Apostles' Creed? The second article begins,

> "And in Jesus Christ, His only Son, our Lord, who was conceived by the Holy Ghost, born of the virgin Mary, suffered under Pontius Pilate, was crucified, dead, and buried; descended into Hades. . . ."

There is no place lower than that! What an awesome descent! But in these words, the Creed affirms that God in Jesus comes all the way down to the bottom of our human condition.

I know where sin and evil are; I know where darkness, sickness, and injustice are. My human question is, Where is God? Because of Jesus, I know where God is. He is wherever sin, suffering, hurting, and sorrow are.

Where is God for you? Be sure that in your thinking you get him down out of heaven and involved with the sin and sorrow and darkness of our world. That is the kind of God he is. God does not sit like Buddha, aloof and in repose, with feet unmuddied and hands unbloodied, uninvolved with the evil of the world. He comes to suffer along with us. The miracle is not that he brings us to where he is; the miracle is that he comes down to where we are, taking to himself our fallen and sinful human nature. He does not work magic from afar; he comes as a human being. He lives and he loves and he cares and he cries—and he dies—like we do. God in Jesus has gone all the way to death on a cross. There is no way back for him. His identification with us is so complete that our human destiny is tied to the very destiny of God.

> Thou dying Lamb, Thy precious blood
> Shall never lose its power
> Till all the ransomed church of God
> Are saved to sin no more.

These words of William Cowper express clearly that the reality of God and our human race are locked together. Leslie Weatherhead wrote that the cross is something like a wedding ring. It is a sign of God's betrothal to us, his covenant commitment to us; it is a sign of his pledge that he will never leave us or forsake us or wipe us out. Oh, that is very good news!

• A Victorious God

Paul tells us that when sin had done its worst to Jesus, when Satan had gone as far as he could go to defeat him, the mighty power of God raised Jesus from the dead and exalted him at the right hand of glory. The good news concerns Jesus, "designated Son of God in power according to the Spirit of holiness by his resurrection from the dead, Jesus Christ our Lord" (v. 4).

If the cross is the sign of God's loving, redeeming involvement with us at the depths of our weakness and sin and evil; if, in the cross of Jesus, God has become one with us in all our humanity; then the resurrection is the sign of God's ultimate triumph over evil, and we are made one with him in his victory. The resurrection means that God's light is greater than the world's darkness. His life is greater than death. God in Jesus has conquered the ultimate foe. He has won for us the victory that we may share. That's what makes the gospel such good news.

Resurrection is not God's drawing Jesus back from the tomb. Resurrection is God's going through the tomb. It is God's conquering of death in a way that robs it of its ultimate power over us. In Jesus, God takes to himself the full weight of the finality of death. And then he triumphs over it in the resurrection. His power is victorious over the worst that can ever happen to us, and it becomes the ground of our hope.

Our belief in this gospel does not indicate that we are naïve about the reality of evil. Our eyes are not closed to the pervasive powers of darkness that control our desperate world. We Christians are not unrealistic about sin and wrong. Rather, we are realistic about the power of God over sin, revealed in the resurrection of Christ. Our hope for ourselves and for our world rests on the reality of God's full entrance into our human situation; it rests on the reality of his suffering, dying, redeeming love; it rests supremely on the power of God that raised Jesus Christ from the dead and enthroned him in glory at God's right hand.

Edwin Lewis tells us that the march of God through the fields of time is not a march of unbroken triumph. God battles for what he gains, and there are losses. But faith is assured of the victory because God has more to give than his adversary—and he gives it!

The life of God is greater than the death of man. The love of God will redeem the hate of man. The light of God will penetrate and illuminate the darkness of man. We know this because, in Jesus, God took into his own experience the darkness, hate, and death of sinful humanity. And when Satan had done the worst he could do, God raised Jesus from the dead.

• Hearing the Gospel for All It's Worth

So the gospel is good news indeed. It is not just good instruction or good advice. Perhaps this is a good time to ask, How do you hear the gospel? What do you hear when you hear it? Does it seem to say, "Try harder. Be kind. Be nice. Keep on trying. Be good"?

A long time ago I read in a book (I think by James Stewart) something like this: *It is a shame that the Christian religion is identified in the minds of many with pious, ethical behavior, together with a vague belief in God, suffused with some esthetic emotionalism and a mild glow of humanitarian benevolence.* That is indeed the way the gospel is perceived in the minds of many people. That perception makes the church seem to be a nice group of people meeting in a nice place having a nice service listening to a nice sermon by a nice pastor telling them to be . . . nicer! It is a case of the bland leading the bland.

My neighbor is not much interested in going to church services because, the few times he went, it seemed the folks were trying to show their goodness in a hypocritical way. I don't agree with him, but I understand how he feels. He doesn't think he needs the church "image" or the good advice he hears or feels there.

But the gospel is not just good advice. Believe me, I know about advice. I am number six of eight children. There were my father and my mother and Harper and Dorothy and Rubena and George and Bill—before I was even born! So I have heard advice all my life: "Be good, be nice, be kind, do right." When my mother spanked me, she would say, "All right, you straighten up now and you be happy!" Good advice! But is that what the gospel is?

I must say that what I need is *not* more good advice. I don't need someone coming around to tell me to be good and be kind and do right and try harder. I have "guilts" enough already! What I do need is *Someone* to come down into the secret arena of my struggle; Someone who knows me from the inside, who is coming from where I am coming from; Someone who loves me and can meet me where I am; Someone who can bring into my life a power and strength greater than my own. If that can ever happen, it is the best news that has ever fallen on my earth-bound, sin-bound heart. And that is precisely the good news of the gospel!

The gospel does not say to me, "Be good." It says God has come in Jesus so I can be saved. It is, then, the word of grace (Rom. 1:5).

The gospel meant everything to Paul. It means everything to me. I cannot think of a worse condition than to live a meaningless life in which I go through the motions of daily existence, knowing that when I die it will have been for nothing. God is bringing to fulfillment his purposes in this world, and I am privileged to be caught up in those great purposes. My life has meaning because it moves within those purposes revealed in Jesus. The sovereign Creator is at work in ways I cannot always discern, but in ways I may trust and in which I may participate.

So with Paul I say I am not ashamed of the gospel. It is the news of God who is at work in our world to fulfill his purposes of grace. It is the news of God who has come in Jesus all the way to where we are, taking to himself our sinful humanity, in order to save us. It is the astounding declaration that the God who raised Jesus from the dead comes to us in him with grace—calling us to belong to him and to participate in his purposes. As sure as God raised Jesus, so sure are our salvation and our hope and our calling.

● Discussion Questions

1. Paul had not been to Rome prior to writing this letter. Judging by Romans 1:1–15, what would you say was his relationship to the church there? Was he trusted by the congregation?
2. If you said, "The coming of Christ was the fulfillment of prophecy," and someone replied, "So what?" what would be your answer?

3. I have related prophecy to the fact that God is always working in human history. We often see God working in the lives of individuals; do you think he is at work in communities, organizations, and nations of the world? If so, cite some evidence of this activity.

4. We hear a great deal of talk in our time about personal goals and personal fulfillment and money and happiness, but we don't hear much about the purpose of human life. What do you think our purpose is?

5. I think many Christians have a hard time accepting the fact that Jesus is just as human as we are. Do you agree? Why is it important that we believe this?

6. Many Christians view the resurrection of Christ as a sign of God's promise of eternal life for us. I believe it is also the decisive proof of God's final triumph over the forces of sin and death. What do you think makes the resurrection of Christ so important for us—if indeed it is?

7. So often people think of Christianity as an effort to be good. Why do you suppose this view is so common? How does this view make the gospel "good advice" instead of good news?

C H A P T E R · 2

Three Great Words of the Gospel

For I am not ashamed of the gospel: it is the power of God for salvation to every one who has faith, to the Jew first and also to the Greek. For in it the righteousness of God is revealed through faith for faith; as it is written, "He who through faith is righteous shall live" (Rom. 1:16–17).

• Salvation: A Many-Splendored Thing

In these verses Paul uses three great words to express the saving power of the gospel in its relation to us. The first one is *salvation*.

"Salvation." What do you think of when you hear that word? I have the feeling that for many of us the word is too small. Our use of it may not be wrong—just limited. We speak of salvation as a synonym for being "born again," or we use it as distinguished from sanctification. Sometimes it is used as in the phrase "my salvation," as though it were a possession, like a ticket to heaven. These uses may be correct to some extent, but I believe they significantly limit what is one of the greatest words of the whole Bible. Salvation is the word that reaches all the way from where God meets us in our human sinful condition to our final glory in heaven. I wish we could stretch the meaning of that word to cover the whole range of God's saving dealings with us.

Wherever New Testament evangelists went, they preached

salvation. Peter and John declared it to the priestly rulers in Jerusalem. Whether Paul was preaching to Jews in Antioch (Acts 13:26) or to a Roman jailer in Philippi (Acts 16:31), he preached salvation. He was confident that—whatever the need, whatever the hunger, through whatever culture it was expressed—the salvation of God was the adequate answer. Paul believed that what people really needed was to be saved. He knew that human need, however expressed, was met in the salvation of God.

Of course, New Testament people did not invent the word. It is a term with a rich heritage from the Old Testament. The Hebrew word for *salvation* variously means safety, security, deliverance, help, and blessing. For Old Testament people, salvation often meant victory in battle. It was the word that spoke of God's deliverance, his provision for their needs, his help, his security. All these ideas are gathered up in the marvelous word *salvation*.

The most vivid picture of salvation in the Old Testament is undoubtedly seen in the story of the Exodus. That was the mighty event in which God delivered Abraham's descendants from their Egyptian bondage, redeeming them to be a nation for himself, a servant people for his saving purposes throughout the whole world. From that time onward, the Israelites knew themselves to be the people of God. Ever afterward, they knew that God is the God who saves—who delivers—his people.

The Exodus story reveals two sides of the meaning of *salvation*. One side is the miracle of deliverance. In bondage the Israelites cried out to God, and God set them free from their enemies in a mighty delivering, redeeming act. The other side (equally as important if not so dramatic) is the idea of blessing. When Egypt was safely behind them, the Israelites found themselves in a new situation with different kinds of problems, needing help in a different way from what they needed as slaves in Egypt. Now they needed food and water and protection. They needed babies and lambs and calves and rain for crops. They needed health and hope. They needed deliverance from discouragement and weariness. They needed courage to carry on the journey. This, too, is part of salvation. God's salvation provided for them in the wilderness no less than it delivered them from Egypt.

New Testament Christians knew the Exodus story; it was the heart of their own heritage. When they preached salvation in Christ, they proclaimed it in the confidence that through his death and resurrection God had wrought the real deliverance pictured and anticipated in the great saving act accomplished at the Red Sea. The saving purpose of God is revealed in Jesus. In him we see that God wills to save, to deliver every person on earth. And in Jesus, God's saving power meets the whole need of the whole person—body, soul, and spirit. When New Testament Christians preached that God is the God who saves, they were saying that God gave himself in Jesus to deliver, to make secure, to heal, to redeem, and to bless us.

It is wonderful to realize how many times and how many ways the words *save, saved,* and *salvation* are used in the New Testament and in what different contexts they are used. Mark tells of a desperate woman, slowly bleeding to death, who said to herself, "If I touch even his garments, I shall be made well [saved]" (Mark 5:28). We would say "healed"; but the people who met Jesus knew that healing is a part of being "saved."

Frightened disciples, swamped in the waves of Galilee, cried out: "Save, Lord; we are perishing" (Matt. 8:25). When Jesus had cast the demons out of the tormented Gerasene, those who witnessed the deliverance told "how he who had been possessed with demons was healed [saved]" (Luke 8:36). Luke tells of a frantic jailer on the verge of suicide, crying in the dark, "Men, what must I do to be saved?" (Acts 16:30). The angel said to Joseph, "You shall call his name Jesus, for he will save his people from their sins" (Matt. 1:21). Jesus said to Zacchaeus, "For the Son of man came to seek and to save the lost" (Luke 19:10).

In our sickness we cry, "Lord, save." Out of our fear and guilt we call, "Lord, save." In our failures, in our despair and lostness, and in our hopelessness, we cry out, "Lord, save." When we lose direction, not knowing which way to turn, and our priorities are confused, we need to be saved. When we are weighted with sinful behaviors and attitudes, we need to be saved. When we are in despair or discouraged or depressed or hurting, we need to be saved. Thomas Merton reminds us that we need to

> be saved from immersion in the sea of lies and passions which is called "the world." And we must be saved above all from that abyss of confusion and absurdity which is our own worldly self. The free son of God must be saved from the conformist slave of fantasy, passion and convention. The creative and mysterious inner self must be delivered from the wasteful, hedonistic and destructive ego that seeks only to cover itself with disguises (*New Seeds of Contemplation*, p. 38).

Oh, we need to be saved, all right. See how that wonderful word stretches out to cover all our need? And Jesus saves!

The word covers not only all our needs, but all our times. Paul indicates in his letters to the Romans and to Titus that salvation is not only something past, but present and future as well. Romans 5:1–2 says:

> Therefore, since we are justified by faith [here he refers to God's gracious saving work in our *past*], we have peace with God through our Lord Jesus Christ. Through him we have obtained access to this grace in which we stand [now he speaks of the salvation that is part of our *present* experience], and we rejoice in our hope of sharing the glory of God [this is the *future* hope of our salvation].

The same dimensions of time are expressed in Titus 2:11–14:

> For the grace of God has appeared for the salvation of all men, training us to renounce irreligion and worldly passions, and to live sober, upright, and godly lives in this world, awaiting our blessed hope, the appearing of the glory of our great God and Savior Jesus Christ, who gave himself for us to redeem us from all iniquity and to purify for himself a people of his own who are zealous for good deeds.

All our needs—needs for deliverance and needs for blessing—and all our times—our past, our present, and our future—are covered in the saving work of God. It is helpful for me to think about it this way:

I have been saved. That is to say, I have experienced the

forgiveness of sins, I have been born of the Holy Spirit, and I have experienced his inward cleansing. This and much more I have received by grace in the past. But there is more.

I am being saved. That is, I now experience the forgiving, cleansing presence of Christ through his Spirit. Present salvation encompasses all that it means to be a Christian. It means the continued forgiving, cleansing, strengthening, sanctifying work of God in my life. It includes my life in the body of believers, the sacraments, the service of God in vocation and in social encounters. In my journey with all its needs, God is saving. The salvation process continues and the saving work of God in my present is as much a part of his salvation as any deliverance I have experienced in the past. And so is the hope of final salvation in heaven!

I will be saved. I will experience the consummation of the salvation of God. I will share the consummation of saving purposes that began with God's gracious involvement with his fallen creation. My present experience of salvation, as well as the salvation of all God's people, will continue till the final renewal of all things at the end of the age.

If someone should ask me, then, "Are you saved?" I could answer, "Have been, am being, or will be?" In any case, my response would be, "Yes, yes, yes!" And all because the gospel is the "power of God for salvation" (Rom. 1:16).

● Righteous God, Righteous People

The next big word is *righteousness.* In the gospel—in the coming of God into our world in Jesus to save us—God's righteousness is revealed, displayed, and made known.

What thoughts does the phrase "the righteousness of God" bring to mind? This was the phrase over which Martin Luther profoundly struggled. He longed to understand the Book of Romans, and it seemed nothing really stood in his way except the phrase "the righteousness of God." He struggled with it because he understood it to mean "that righteousness whereby God is righteous and deals righteously in punishing the unrighteous."

I think the word *righteousness* troubles us as well. Part of our problem may be our language. *Righteousness* is a translation of a Greek word that also means justification. Paul's Greek readers understood that to be "righteous" is to be just; to "justify" is to righteous-ify; justification is the same as righteous-ification. (Can't you hear Paul dictating Romans 5? "Therefore, since we are righteousified by faith . . .") Thus part of our problem is our Western way of thinking. When we say someone is righteous, we think that person has high morals and character; we suppose the person is honest and pure—maybe even a bit stuffy. When we say that God is righteous, we mean that he is pure and holy and without sin or deceit—totally upright. It's difficult for us to imagine how a human being could be righteous in this sense.

But in Paul's religious vocabulary, *righteousness* meant not so much a moral quality of character as an act or an activity. It was not a passive word, but a living and active one. When Paul said that in the gospel "the righteousness of God is revealed," he did not mean that it was becoming obvious to all that God is just and holy. He meant that a divine activity was taking place in Christ Jesus; God was openly putting things and persons to rights.

In the Old Testament, the Hebrew word translated *righteous* has the primary meaning of "to be in the right" rather than "to be righteous." The word is used also to mean "to vindicate, " or "to give redress" to a person who has suffered wrong. For example, a judge or a ruler was thought to be righteous, not so much for upholding impartial standards of justice, as for vindicating the cause of those who had been wronged. If a ruler undertook the cause of the poor, the orphans, the widows, and those who had been oppressed by the system, that ruler was called righteous. His righteousness was revealed in "putting right," or justifying, those who were victims of evil.

In Jesus, God is doing the same thing. He is reaching out to put right what is wrong. He comes to undertake the cause of the oppressed (namely, us), to stand up for the poor (namely, us), and to bring deliverance to those who cannot help themselves (namely, us). The Gospels depict Jesus as one who comes to put right what is wrong, to straighten out what is messed up, to liberate, to free, to put things and people right!

The vindication of right involves finally a real righteousness on the part of those who are delivered. A people must be delivered not only from wrongful oppression, but from their own inward sin as well: They must become a *righteous* people in our normal sense of the word. But righteousness is not primarily an attribute of character. It is the holy activity whereby, in faithfulness to his covenant, God asserts what is right and delivers his fallen creatures from their bondage to sin and Satan.

Paul proclaims that this righteous activity of God is revealed in the life, death, and resurrection of Jesus Christ our Lord. In the Christ event, God is saving and redeeming his people, delivering them (namely, us) from the power of evil.

Well, then, what about righteousness in us? What does the Bible mean when it says we must be righteous? In this connection, it describes a relationship, not an activity. God in righteousness offers us salvation and redemption. We are considered righteous when we respond to this new relationship that God in mercy has established in Christ. Our righteousness is our response to God's action. So when the Bible refers to a *righteous* person, it does not signify a perfect person with flawless character. There are none. Remember righteous Abraham or righteous Lot or righteous Moses or Joshua or David? Their righteousness did not consist of their law-abiding lives or moral achievements, but of their response to God, who called them into relationship with himself. They said yes to God, both to his judgment and his forgiveness, and were brought into right relationship with him.

Where does righteousness begin for us? It began when God acted in Jesus to set us free, to deliver us, to make us his own. When we respond to him with the Yes of our hearts, we enter into right relationship with him, and we become righteous.

Again, let me emphasize that *righteousness* is not primarily a word of character. It does not mean we suddenly receive a perfect character. It means we are, by God's grace, put to rights with him. Within that righteous relationship, God works by his Spirit to make us *righteous* in our ordinary sense of the word. He works to produce in us "the fruits of righteousness which come through Jesus Christ, to the glory and praise of God" (Phil. 1:11).

● Living in Faith

The Bible word for a person's whole life response to Jesus is *faith*. That is our next big word of the gospel. Paul is not using the word here to indicate a certain set of beliefs, as when we speak of "the Christian faith"; nor is he using it as we do when we refer to the intellectual acceptance of something as true. In Romans 1:16–17, *faith* means saving faith. Paul believed that *faith* is an attitude of perfect trust in God's mercy or grace. It is complete reliance upon God, not on one's own merit or effort, to gain salvation. It is the disposition of our own hearts that answers to God's loving disposition toward us. It is the act of receiving into ourselves the love of God, receiving it in the only way that love can ever be received—with humility and thankfulness.

On the one hand, a person of faith has confidence in God's goodness and love revealed in Jesus Christ. A Christian's faith is faith *in* Someone. Faith does not initiate anything; faith is a personal response to the fact about God revealed in Christ. I think that is why the Christian church has always had such a concern for church history and archaeology. The ground of our faith is not a vacuum filled with images and events born of our own fantasies. The real Jesus has revealed the real God, and we begin our life of faith by trusting that fact of history.

On the other hand, *faith* is our awareness of our own lack of righteousness and our inability to achieve it on our own. In this respect, faith is related to the spirit of humility and repentance. It is an attitude toward God that involves a proper attitude toward ourselves. Our self-dependency and self-serving are shut out. God in love offers himself to us, and faith is the response of our lives to his gracious offer. It involves a turning away from ourselves to receive what he has to give us. C. H. Dodd once wrote that faith is *to cease from all assertion of self and make room for the divine initiative.* This is an important yet neglected aspect of faith.

What changed my life was the realization of what God had already done. I did not make it true by believing it; it was already true. I could not make it false by disbelieving it; it was already true. What I needed to do was accept it, believe it, and act on it by letting God act in me.

God says Yes to us in Jesus. Faith is the Yes of our hearts in response to him. In this sense, to "have faith" means to hear, to listen, to obey, to respond, and to trust the Word of God in Jesus that meets us in the gospel. Thank God, there are no built-in limits to his Word. The gospel is "the power of God for salvation to *every one* who has faith" (Rom. 1:16).

Faith is not a subtle form of works; it does not consist of our spiritual efforts or strainings to lay hold of God and make ourselves right with him. In old, familiar words, it is "letting go and letting God." His righteousness has been revealed; his salvation has been offered in Christ. Can we believe it?

● Discussion Questions

1. How would you define *salvation?* Do you gain any new insights about this word from the chapter? To me, it means much more than being saved from sin. What do you think? In what sense is the sanctifying work of God part of his saving work in our lives?
2. Discuss the idea that salvation is past, present, and future.
3. When we say that God is righteous, what do we usually mean? Discuss how being righteous is different from being good. Discuss *righteousness* as an action word.
4. I have used the word *faith* in this chapter to mean saving faith. What are some other dimensions or other kinds of faith? Do all kinds of faith have some things in common? Gives examples.
5. How would you respond to the question, "What does it mean to believe the gospel, or to have faith in Christ?"

C H A P T E R · 3

Justification
by Faith

For the wrath of God is revealed from heaven against all ungodliness
and wickedness of men who by their wickedness suppress the
truth. . . .

You have no excuse, O man, whoever you are, when you judge
another; for in passing judgment upon him you condemn yourself,
because you, the judge, are doing the very same things. . . .

There is no distinction; since all have sinned and fall short of the
glory of God, they are justified by his grace as a gift, through the
redemption which is in Christ Jesus, . . .

Therefore, since we are justified by faith, we have peace with God
through our Lord Jesus Christ. Through him we have obtained access
to this grace in which we stand, and we rejoice in our hope of sharing
the glory of God (Rom. 1:18; 2:1; 3:22–24; 5:1–2).

● The Bible begins with the premise that we are sinners.
Something is wrong with us. If what is the matter with us is the
result of our psychological determinisms or our physiological
givens, if we are the result of how our monitor genes function, or
if we are the way we are because of our economic situation or
family environment, then we can be cured by the right medicine, a
good education, a better job, or professional counseling—or a
couple of million more years of evolutionary development.
(Something in me says, "I can't wait!")

The Bible says that what is wrong with us is sin. *Sin* is a special
kind of word. It isn't found in books on history or sociology or

psychology or economics. It is a religious word. Actually, to call persons sinners is to give them a sort of backhanded compliment. It means that such persons are not only related to their environment or other persons or their own chemistry; they are related to God, too. From the Word of God we understand that the human creature is human because of a unique relationship with God. A human being does not find meaning or fulfillment in the world of things or in the world of nature or even in the world of other persons. Ultimately they are found only in relationship with God. The human person is created in the image of God—the only creature to whom God speaks, the only one with whom God enters into dialogue and calls into creative fellowship and partnership. A human being is the only creature who can respond to God in responsible, loving obedience.

The premise of the Bible story is that the first human couple, instead of responding in trustful obedience, acted in prideful disobedience and broke this open, loving relationship. The Bible understands humanity's true situation to be one of both glory and misery. Each man and woman is both created in the image of God and fallen, both potential saint and compulsive sinner.

● Good News ... and Bad News

We have said the gospel is good news in that it explains that the righteousness of God has been revealed to save us. Perhaps this is the time to say that the gospel is good news because, first of all, it is bad news. In Romans 1:18 and following, Paul declares that the judgment of God is on the sin of mankind: "For the wrath of God is revealed from heaven against all ungodliness and wickedness of men who by their wickedness suppress the truth." "The wrath of God" does not mean fitful passion and anger. It is his holy revulsion against all that is contradictory to his holiness. It is the positive outgoing of divine displeasure against sin. In Emil Brunner's descriptive phrase, God's wrath is the "adverse wind" of the divine will, which is felt by anyone who runs against it.

God's wrath is related to the moral order of the universe as the negative side of God's laws. There is a moral law in this world; if we break that law, we come under its penalty, under the wrath of God. In this sense, we really do not break the laws of God, we illustrate them—we break ourselves upon them. The wrath of God has been called the inevitable punishment of sin. Suffering follows sin; this is the wrath of God.

I think more must be said than this, because the wrath of God is a terrible thing. He will not be indifferent to the destruction of his creation and the rejection of his holy will. The awful condition of our human situation in the world is not simply the result of our poor choices and bad behavior; it exposes our human situation apart from God and under the wrath of God.

Beginning with Romans 1:18 and continuing through 3:20, Paul describes in most graphic and inelegant language the sinful human situation. He clearly demonstrates our desperate need of the righteousness of God. He first talks about the sin of the Gentile world. The key phrase is 1:21, "for although they knew God they did not honor him as God or give thanks to him." I believe this to be the fundamental sin of mankind: the unwillingness to let God be God, to accept the role of the thankful creature under the sovereignty of the Creator. What is wrong with us is our fundamental will to autonomy. We know that what is "automatic" acts by itself. That is the way we wish to be. We will to be self-sovereign.

Every human being was created in a wondrous and delicate balance—a part of God's creation, at home in the environment, and related to the animal world. (Actually, though some furniture arrangement is called for, it takes about the same effort to run a home as it takes to run a zoo. At times, one wonders which is which!) The human person is part of the created world. But he is above it while belonging to it. He is lord of creation, as we see when Adam names the animals and tends the garden. But he is to exercise his lordship as the responsible steward of God. He has been called into creative partnership with the creator God to care for creation in responsible stewardship. Part of creation . . . lord of creation . . . accountable steward of creation—that is the wondrous and delicate balance.

God gave us dominion. Our sin is that we exercise it apart from responsible, creative partnership with God. We fulfill our own will and exploit the created order for our own selfish ends. This is why we are witnessing the frightening acceleration of consumption and destruction of our resources. The problem is not that we exercise dominion under God; it is that we pursue exploitation under self.

The Book of Genesis tells how the original perversion of our primary God-relationship led to the perversion of all human relationships. The biblical view is that creation is a beautiful thing, but spoiled. What has spoiled it is sin; and somewhere near the heart of sin is self-sovereignty, self-will. The first human couple found themselves at odds with their Creator. Labor, instead of being a blessing, became their curse. Children were born to them in pain and sorrow. In their guilt, the parents quarreled, the children murdered, and the environment became diseased.

As children of fallen Adam, we continue to live and love in opposition to God's order. God is off the throne of our lives, self is on the throne, and this monstrous inversion affects the whole of our existence.

Paul speaks of this in terms of mankind's fatal exchange. "The glory of the immortal God" was exchanged "for images resembling mortal man or birds or animals or reptiles" (Rom. 1:23); "they exchanged the truth about God for a lie and worshiped and served the creature rather than the Creator" (1:25); and men and women "exchanged natural relations for unnatural . . . consumed with passion for one another . . . committing shameless acts" (1:26–27). See the awful process of disruption! Our break with God leads inevitably to destructive relations with one another and with our world. The results are idolatry, immorality, and animosity of all kinds; false religion, defiled bodies, and a fractured social structure; impurity, dishonorable passions, and base minds. These are more than the natural or inevitable consequences of bad behavior; they are the awesome expressions of the wrath of God, the God who "gave them up" (1:24, 26, 28).

● The Sins of Religious People

Beginning with Romans 2, Paul adds another disturbing and very significant dimension to the reality of our fallen, sinful condition: "You have no excuse, O man, whoever you are, when you judge another." He goes on to disclose the sin of the Jews or the religious people of any day. If the basic sin of mankind is the unwillingness to let God be God, the basic sin of religious folk is spiritual or moral pride, which leads to the spirit of judgment. We have heard of pride of race, pride of place, pride of face, and pride of grace. However the pride is defined, Paul confronts it with profound seriousness. He speaks of those who know the law, who have the proper religious heritage, who are "in the know," who are the teachers of religious ideals, who yet subvert these advantages to their own destruction.

We thus learn that sin is all-pervasive. We can neither condone the sins of men nor judge them, for we are enmeshed in the fallen structure of our social existence. What irreligious people do in an open and flagrant way, religious people can do in a refined and subtle way. The discerning God discloses and judges such hypocrisy. Without question, the sins of irreligious people are awful in their depth and consequence. But, also without question, the "un-sins" of the "un-sinners" can lead to pride, self-righteousness, and censoriousness, which are just as awful in their depth and consequence.

Well, we know what the conclusion is. All of us, Jew and Gentile, good folk and bad folk, them and us, "have sinned" and have fallen "short of the glory of God" (Rom. 3:23). The distressing analysis of the religious condition of mankind applies to all of us; "there is no distinction" (Rom. 3:22). We are all morally and spiritually bankrupt. In John Knox's words, "Paul sees all men as guilty before God and slaves of evil impulses—thus under a righteous condemnation which they cannot evade, and held captive by a demonic power of evil which they cannot successfully resist and from whose grasp they cannot escape."

I heard of a nonreligious man who wandered off the sidewalk

into the sanctuary of a cathedral one Sunday morning just in time to hear the congregation confess in unison: "We have left undone those things which we ought to have done and we have done those things which we ought not to have done." *I don't know what's going on here,* he said to himself. *But at last I have found my crowd.* We are all part of that crowd: responsible sinners who need forgiveness, helpless sinners who need deliverance.

• Good News for Sinners

It is time to hear the gospel. In full awareness of the awesome reality of human sinfulness, Paul proclaims the wondrous truth of justification by faith: "For there is no distinction; since all have sinned and fall short of the glory of God, they are justified by his grace as a gift, through the redemption which is in Christ Jesus. . . . it was to prove at the present time that he himself is righteous and that he justifies him who has faith in Jesus" (Rom. 3:22–24, 26). What we cannot do, God—in infinite, costly, redeeming love—does for us. Broken and crippled by our fall, we cannot save ourselves. Deliverance must come from somewhere else. And it does. The initiative passes to God, and he takes it. "While we were yet helpless, at the right time Christ died for the ungodly" (5:6). "While we were enemies we were reconciled to God by the death of his Son" (5:10). At the point of sin, at the point of guilt, in our inability and alienation we are justified by his grace. Salvation is his gift to us. God meets us in Christ and, because of our faith, declares us to be in right relationship with him. God greets us as sinners and meets us in grace.

The saving truth of justification by faith is difficult to believe. It is a hard doctrine to accept, especially for us good people. On the one hand, it seems too easy. Does God in Christ forgive all our sins and put us right with him just because we believe something? On the other hand, it is actually too good to be true. It is like the other free gifts we don't accept because we know that somewhere in the deal is some fine print that will require us to pay.

I also think the word *justification* gives us difficulty because of the way we use it in everyday life. When I "justify" myself, I think of all the reasons why I did what I did, why I couldn't actually have done differently, and why you would have done the same thing or worse if you had been in my situation. We all maintain some balance of guilt and goodness. I may not go to church as much as some folks think I should; but there are lots of things I do for the kingdom that they don't know about. I may not give as much in the offering as some do; but at least I don't make a show of my piety. Next year we will send Christmas cards to the people we didn't send to this year because we didn't know they were going to send one to us. This thinking conveniently "justifies" what we do.

We do this even when we apologize. If we hurt someone's feelings or disappoint someone, we ask their forgiveness in such a way as to keep our egos intact: "I'm so sorry; please forgive me. That was not like me; I just wasn't myself; I'm really not like that at all; I'm terribly sorry; I just hate myself." When this sort of thing is handled in the right way (some of us have made it an art), the person who has been hurt or disappointed ends up feeling guilty for being hurt! There is neither true confession nor true forgiveness in this effort to maintain the balance of guilt and goodness.

The trouble is that we carry the pattern over into our relationships with God. A minister told me about a time he was invited to speak at the church of a pastor friend of his. His friend met him at the plane, and on the way to the parsonage my friend Bill said something about someone they both knew and was immediately aware that it was an inappropriate and hurtful thing to say. "Oh, I'm so sorry," he stammered. "I shouldn't have said that. I didn't mean to be hurtful. Please forgive me."

His pastor friend said, "I understand, Bill. I know you didn't mean to hurt. It's okay. I forgive you."

When they got to the house and were getting ready to eat, Bill said, "Man, I really am sorry. I shouldn't have done that."

His friend said, "That's okay, Bill. I really understand and really believe you, and I forgive you."

That night after church the same conversation was repeated, and again on the way to the airport. Finally, the pastor turned to him and said, "Will you shut up? You have apologized; you have been sorry; you have asked me to forgive you. I have forgiven you. Now, will you let me forgive you or not?"

I imagine that as Bill walked through the gate to the ramp, he turned to say once more, "I really am sorry, brother. Forgive me!"

How hard to accept free forgiveness! As Paul Tillich put it, if we have not acted worthily, we can at least be terribly sorry.

For all our talk of the centrality of justification by faith, it is painfully difficult to give up our defenses and excuses and let ourselves be forgiven. We either make our sins of no account or make ourselves of no account. But it seems we *must* do something more than just be made right with God.

Years ago, when I was a college chaplain, a student went home for Christmas vacation and had an abortion. Some weeks into the new term, we found ourselves in my office talking about it. We would talk awhile, and she would say, "But it is no big thing." More talk and again, "No big thing."

"Have you asked the Lord to forgive you?"

"Of course."

"Do you believe he does?"

"Well, he says he does. . . . But it is no big thing."

Several years later, another student and I were talking about the same kind of situation. She thought a young man loved her; but when he learned that she was pregnant, he said, "Thanks, but no thanks. I'll see you around."

She was devastated. She cried, prayed, thought, talked, pondered, cried, and prayed some more. She finally decided to have an abortion, too. She came to see me afterward. "I killed my baby," she cried. We talked some more. "I killed my baby."

"Have you asked the Lord to forgive you?"

"Oh, every hour on the hour!"

"Do you believe he does?"

"Well, he says he does. . . . " (The words had a familiar sound.)

It is not my intention to discuss the abortion issue here. It is my intention to show how we deal with guilt and forgiveness. Both persons experienced guilt that was real to them. Both had asked for God's forgiveness. Neither had experienced the reality of it because each was handling guilt in some way other than the good old way of repentance, confession, and the joyful acceptance of God's full, free forgiveness. One was saying, "What I did was not all that bad after all." So there was no real forgiveness, only self-justification. The other was saying, "I am so bad there is no hope for me." So there was no real forgiveness, only self-condemnation.

I am thankful that for them both, full and free forgiveness was finally experienced—but not without some serious talks about what justification really means.

I once talked to a student who said that when he was a child and did something wrong, his mother told him to tell the Lord about it and accept his forgiveness. No problem: little forgiveness for little sins. But when he grew up and got in some real trouble that caused profound guilt, he discovered that he still had a child's view of forgiveness. He believed in forgiveness—oh, yes—but it was thin and trivial, good only for little sins. Simply to confess and believe Christ for forgiveness and full restoration for deep and profound and involved guilt did not seem possible.

• Restored to Right Relation

The great good news of the gospel is that God breaks through all our defenses and rationalizations and self-justifications and self-condemnations to set us right with himself by faith.

Remember the old story of the lady who had her portrait painted? After the final sitting, the artist presented her with the finished work. She beheld the likeness of herself, and her countenance fell. She cried out, "Oh, that doesn't do me justice!"

"Madam, you don't need justice—you need mercy!"

Just so! God would confound our moral logic and our self-styled goodness; he would break through our protected balance of guilt and goodness; he would confront us with his love and make us right with himself, by himself. Justification by faith is not our hopeless struggle to achieve the impossible task of pleasing God; it is accepting, just as we are, the offer of his love, in the confidence that, instead of pouring out the judgments of outraged holiness, God pours out healing waters of forgiving love and treats us as though we had never been away. It is our saying, "I'm wrong," and God's saying, "You're right."

The sinner is righteous. In what way? The sinner is righteous because God has declared it so. How can God say what is not really true at all? Surely the sinner is not "righteous"!

But it is so because righteousness is not something we have; it is a new, healing, saving, forgiving relationship that we receive from God in Christ. Remember what we learned in chapter 2. Faith is not a mental affirmation or acceptance of some statement of God; it is the opening of our whole hearts to his initiative of grace, the trustful reliance upon him and not ourselves. This makes our righteousness a fact.

William Barclay says that if God justifies sinners, it does not mean he finds reasons to prove that they were right. It means that God reckons us not as his enemies, but as his friends. To be *justified* is to enter into a right relationship with God, based not on our efforts or claims or supposed goodness, but on our humble acceptance of his gift of himself to us in Jesus.

When Paul speaks of the person who is just or righteous, he means the person who is in a right relationship with God. That relationship cannot be won; it can only be accepted. God's justifying word is not simply a forensic exercise; he does not work magic, nor does he declare to be true what is not true. What he does do is forgive and restore us to himself. What he will do is "welcome, pardon, cleanse, relieve." So,

> Because Thy promise I believe,
> O Lamb of God, I come, I come.
> —*Charlotte Elliott*

• Discussion Questions

1. We know that God does not become angry as people do. What do you think the "wrath of God" means? What is wrong with the idea that God is angry and will judge us, but Jesus loves us and died for us and will save us?

2. I suggest that the fundamental sin of mankind is self-sovereignty. What would you say is at the very heart of the sin of mankind?

3. What do you think is meant by the "image of God" in man? I think it is necessary to hold together the truth of the divine image of God in man and man's fallenness. What happens when we remove or minimize either one?

4. I hold that in spite of all our words to the contrary, we really think that sins of the flesh are worse than sins of the spirit. Would you agree? Discuss.

5. Why do you think it is so hard to ask for and receive forgiveness we do not deserve?

6. In the illustration of the two who experienced real guilt, one reacted one way and the other reacted another way. How do you respond to them? Was one reaction more proper than the other?

7. Discuss the idea that forgiveness is not just a one-time event, but the beginning of an ongoing and truly open relationship with God.

C H A P T E R · 4
Reconciliation

While we were yet helpless, at the right time Christ died for the ungodly. Why, one will hardly die for a righteous man—though perhaps for a good man one will dare even to die. But God shows his love for us in that while we were yet sinners Christ died for us. Since, therefore, we are now justified by his blood, much more shall we be saved by him from the wrath of God. For if while we were enemies we were reconciled to God by the death of his Son, much more, now that we are reconciled, shall we be saved by his life. Not only so, but we also rejoice in God through our Lord Jesus Christ, through whom we have now received our reconciliation (Rom. 5:6–11).

● The Bible contains several pictures or *metaphors* that reveal the relationships between God and man. For instance, God is shown as Creator and man as the creature; God is revealed as moral ruler of the world and man as responsible subject. Another metaphor is the Father-son or Parent-child bond. It is a picture of family relationships. If justification brings us into the courtroom where the judge pardons the guilty prisoner, reconciliation brings us into the family where suffering love overcomes guilt and alienation and restores open, loving fellowship. James S. Stewart has written that the worst of sin's consequences is alienation from God. Even though there may be no conscious or deliberate intention to offend God, something happens to our relationship with God when we sin. We become aware of alienation, loneliness, and estrangement.

• Four Pictures of Broken Relationships

The truth is that we live in a world of broken relationships. The biblical understanding of our separated condition is profoundly expressed in the four great stories of Genesis 1–11. These narratives of the Garden, the Brothers, the Flood, and the Tower are variations on the theme of alienation. They reveal the extent of the brokenness of our relationship with God and our consequent alienation from one another and from our environment.

In the Garden of Eden the fundamental relationship with God is broken through disobedience, producing guilt. The human couple created for fellowship with God, who walked and talked with him in the cool of the day, now hide from his presence and cover their nakedness in fear. After naming the animals (with whom he found no real fellowship), Adam had greeted Eve with a joyful cry of recognition and identity, as bone of his bone, flesh of his flesh. The two had been one in fellowship and love, open to each other before their Creator. But when confronted with the reality of his disobedience, the man blames his partner and God, speaking of "the woman whom thou gavest to be with me . . ." (Gen. 3:12). The two who had been side by side are pitted against each other in accusation and blame. The parents quarrel; the children murder. Instead of the bonding of community there is fratricide.

The flow of alienation even reaches to the environment. The ground is cursed (Gen. 3:17). Man must force a living from the resistant earth. What a picture: estrangement from God, alienation between the human pair, murder between the children, and disharmony with the very soil that was the origin of their being.

The Flood narrative introduces a new dimension into this destructive pattern of alienation: the dimension of judgment. The Flood comes to destroy them all, yet there is grace in the rescue of Noah and his family who, in spite of their own "fall," are the recipients of covenant mercy and who see in the rainbow the everlasting commitment of God to his human creatures.

The Tower of Babel becomes the symbol of man's desire to make his own name great, his propensity to create a society totally apart from the will and the sovereignty of God. "Let us make a name for ourselves," the builders say (Gen. 11:4). No mention of God or of his purposes defines the goals or the limits of this prideful society. The end, of course, is confusion, misunderstanding, isolation, mutual mistrust, and hostility.

● The Consequences of Broken Relations

Paul knew these stories better than we do. He knew the awful depths of alienation and suspicion caused by the guilt that separates us from our Maker, our meaning, and ourselves. This primal guilt fosters our separation from one another and from our environment; it destroys our trust in God and in one another. Moral failure and sin produce the guilt that brings estrangement. Estrangement produces loneliness and alienation. The isolation often breeds hopelessness, which produces recklessness, which then becomes the hostility so often acted out in rebellion.

Here is an example that I have seen more than once: In class I give an assignment due the following Wednesday. One of the students does not do it and so does not show up in class that day. I say, "We are going to have a quiz over this material on Friday, so be sure to review it carefully." But the absent student does not hear this, and his friends don't tell him about it.

On Friday, here he comes, a little more cheerful than normal, covering his guilt for not doing the assignment and for missing class—only to be confronted with a quiz that he didn't know he was going to have over material he has not read. He looks at the quiz, flushes with guilt and anger, slaps it down on the desk, and stalks out of the room, muttering to himself, "This isn't fair. How was I supposed to know? Welch is the stupidest teacher in this whole stupid college. Anyhow, what do I care!"

The simple episode illustrates our human condition in relation to God and to one another: guilt, anger, alienation, hostility. All the while the student really wants to be back "in the family," at peace with himself, his professor, his classwork, and his peers.

He is not alone. You bought stuff you could not really afford, and so you are angry with your husband, who doesn't even know you have it. Or you are angry with your wife about things you have done or bought, and she doesn't have the slightest idea what is going on. You have broken the family code and are angry with your parents; they are wondering what is the matter with you, knowing nothing of your private guilt. How long shall we make this list of examples? It could be *very* long.

I think most persons do not sin willfully in the sense of making a deliberate choice to go away from God. They sin more like sheep going astray, following their desires, mostly in ignorance and weakness. But such ignorance and weakness do not stand condemned. It is the process of covering, justifying, rationalizing, and excusing that is so destructive. Because we rationalize and defend our weakness and guilt, we fall into alienation, which is the source of much hostility and rebellion. I do not believe that all our alienation and estrangement from one another is guilt-based, but much of it is. Underneath our destructive attitudes and behaviors is a sense of alienation and isolation from God. We may not even think of ourselves as separated from God. *God* may not even be in our working vocabulary! But it is true nonetheless. We live in a world of broken human relationships, which ultimately reflect our loss of fellowship with God.

• Healing for Our Brokenness

Now the good news of the gospel is that God comes to us in Jesus to penetrate our guilty isolation and alienation, saying to us, "I love you." God takes the initiative to reach us. It seems that God has done that all along. In the Garden, he provided covering for the guilty, naked pair. A protecting mark was put on Cain in spite of his wickedness. The Flood of judgment was followed by the rainbow of hope. The separation and misunderstanding that frustrated the building of the Tower of Babel led to God's choice of Abraham, the father of the people through whom the Savior of the world would come.

So what Paul says in Romans is in continuity with the reconciling action of God through all the history of mankind's sin and alienation: "While we were yet helpless . . . Christ died. . . . While we were yet sinners Christ died for us. . . . While we were enemies we were reconciled to God by the death of his Son" (5:6, 8, 10). Do we realize that God is the reconciling God, who comes into our isolation and defensiveness to bring us back into his fellowship where we want to be?

I talked with a woman at a retreat who said, "My church doesn't love me. They just want me to be good and do right. If I act the way they want me to, they love me; but when I don't, they would rather I didn't come around."

A student of my wife sat on our couch one night and said, "My parents don't love me. They just love my soul. If I am late coming in with the car, they never ask if I had any trouble or if I am all right. They are just mad that I broke the rule and are worried about the car."

J. S. Whale has reminded us that some religions know of no divine welcome for the sinner until he has ceased to be one. They would first make him righteous and then welcome him to God. But God in Christ first welcomes the sinner—and so makes him repentant and redeems him. One form of religion demands newness of life; the other imparts it.

I believe this is the only answer to the terrible paradox that grips us. Our weakness and our inability to cope with our sins draw us to Christ; yet we feel that we must overcome these very things we cannot overcome in order to come to Christ, who alone can free us. At one and the same time, then, we are drawn to Christ and driven from him. We are both attracted and repelled. Could it be that we are not so much repelled by Christ himself as we are by our own expectations and those of the ones around us? Do we feel threatened by other people's expectations that we must quit our sinning and straighten up our lives before we can come to Christ and be saved?

● God Takes the Initiative

In changeless and unwearying love, God has taken the initiative to reach us. He has broken into the atmosphere of our hostility and has thrown down every estranging barrier that guilt, hopelessness, and dull resentment can erect. The willing God seeks to bring unwilling man into his holy fellowship. This is the heart of the gospel. At the cross, God in Jesus "has broken every barrier down." Anything that still separates us from him is not on his side.

The willing God seeks unwilling man. He does not offer us the forgiveness of the cross *after* we come to him in contrition and remorse. He holds out to us the forgiveness of the cross as the initial gesture. This is the prevenient grace of God, who in Christ at Calvary deals with our sin in his forgiving love. Our repentance does not generate the forgiving activity of God. His offer of forgiveness makes our repentance a response to his loving initiative. It means that our repentance does not have to be crushing self-humiliation; rather, we can open our repentant hearts to him in self-forgetful love. We are not forced to despise ourselves or berate ourselves. We can forget ourselves in his reconciling love.

Let's say a child deeply offends a parent. The parent in love forgives the child, then stays close in care and openness. Years later, the child, now awakened to the depth and reality of the offense, returns to ask forgiveness again. The parent replies, "I forgave you long ago." Is that the way it is with the forgiveness of God? I believe it is. In Jesus on the cross, God has already forgiven us. So forgiveness is not a new decision God makes at the time we come to him to ask. We could not come to him unless he had first come to us to reconcile us to himself.

This is not a form of cheap grace. It is costly to reconcile, and it is costly to be reconciled. But if any kind of personal estrangement or alienation is ever to be healed, one party must take the initiative in the restoration. This party assumes the burden, accepts the weight of the situation, and thus makes it possible for the other to come back without being destroyed.

If the student who in shame and anger stalks out of the classroom is ever to be restored to fellowship with me, I must take the initiative and say to him, "Look, I love you. Let's work this out." I must do it in such a way that he doesn't have to crawl back into the room next day and publicly humiliate himself to show his sincerity or repentance. That would be an overwhelming obstacle to the very reconciliation that we both desire.

With regard to our guilt and sin, we are wrong and God is right. In fact, we are totally wrong and God is totally right. The wonder of the reconciliating love of God is that he takes to himself the burden, the shame, the alienation, the weight of it all so that when we come to him we are not destroyed, but set free. The cross enables us to respond to him in free and self-forgetful love, with joy instead of crushing self-humiliation.

Think of reconciliation in this way: Every one of us has been hurt. Each of us has been affected by the sinfulness of our human situation. And we pass it along; we keep the cycle of alienation going. The abused become the abusers; the hurt become the hurters. Along life's way, I have felt the pain of sin and sorrow and misunderstanding and disappointment. Worse yet, like all other children of Adam, I have passed it on. I have hurt and disappointed others. They share the pain of my guilt and failure. The cycle has been continuous and inevitable since sin first entered our human situation.

Then Jesus came. He received the hurts and wounds and disappointments, the guilts and fears and destructiveness that had been passed on through the ages. He received and received—even to death. But he never passed them on! He has broken the chain of inevitability and, by his death, has opened the door to freedom. God has raised him from the dead so that the cycle of estrangement is nullified. We are reconciled to God.

If, as Stewart says, the worst of sin's consequences is alienation, then the best of the gospel news is that God has overstepped our self-imposed boundaries and entered our guilty, defensive hearts with the healing word, "I love you. Be reconciled to me." God has done this in Jesus. He has died for us. We do not have to take upon ourselves all the weight of guilt and repentance for our sins. We can "lay our sins on Jesus." We are not called to hate ourselves or grovel in sorrow to demonstrate our sinfulness or our sincerity. We can respond to him in love and trust. We can lay down our arms without being destroyed.

The Father's heart beats for reconciliation. Are we reconciled persons? Do we understand that there aren't any barriers on God's side? God is not waiting for us to come and please him; he is waiting for us to open up the doors we have locked, to swing wide the gates we have barricaded, to take down the fences we have built—and let him in. We can come home in freedom, for our shame has been borne by the One who invites us.

● Discussion Questions

1. Suggest if you can some Bible images or metaphors or pictures of the relationship between God and mankind other than those mentioned in this chapter.
2. Do you agree that the worst of sin's consequences is alienation from God? Discuss.
3. What personal examples come to mind of the guilt-defensiveness-hostility process mentioned in the chapter?
4. I emphasize God's initiative in reconciliation. Have I overstated or understated our need to demonstrate repentance?
5. Do you think other people make it harder to come to Christ than Christ does? Discuss.
6. I suggest that God in Christ forgives us in such a way that we do not have to hate ourselves or be crushed in the process. Discuss.
7. What are some ways our genuine reconciliation with God will affect our reconciliation with others? What about being reconciled to God's providences in our lives, or to his demands?

CHAPTER · 5
Dying With Christ

What shall we say then? Are we to continue in sin that grace may abound? By no means! How can we who died to sin still live in it? Do you not know that all of us who have been baptized into Christ Jesus were baptized into his death? We were buried therefore with him by baptism into death, so that as Christ was raised from the dead by the glory of the Father, we too might walk in newness of life.

For if we have been united with him in a death like his, we shall certainly be united with him in a resurrection like his. We know that our old self was crucified with him so that the sinful body might be destroyed, and we might no longer be enslaved to sin. For he who has died is freed from sin. But if we have died with Christ, we believe that we shall also live with him. For we know that Christ being raised from the dead will never die again; death no longer has dominion over him. The death he died he died to sin, once for all, but the life he lives he lives to God. So you also must consider yourselves dead to sin and alive to God in Christ Jesus (Rom. 6:1–11).

● Paul's transition question is significant. He has talked about our sin and about the wondrous love of God that meets us with justifying, reconciling grace. He has explained that we are freed from our hopeless struggle to achieve the impossible task of pleasing God. He has described how God comes to us, breaking through the barriers we have made, saying to us in Jesus, "I love you." For this reason, he says, we "have peace with God through our Lord Jesus Christ. . . . access to this grace . . . and we rejoice in our hope of sharing the glory of God. More than that, we rejoice in our suffering. . . . " We are able to endure in hope "because God's love has been poured into our hearts through the Holy Spirit which has been given to us" (Rom. 5:1–5). What a gospel!

Then comes the question of 6:1, "What shall we say then? Are we to continue in sin that grace may abound?" To us it sounds absurd. Perhaps Paul meant it to sound that way so that he could emphasize his point. Still, the question doesn't go away. It didn't for him and it doesn't for us. However interpreted, it expresses a fundamental issue: Can the sinner be forgiven and that's that? There is evidently more to be said—and Paul takes the rest of Romans to say it. He draws out the deeper implications of justification and reconciliation.

In my view, Paul's questioners understood something about justification, but they did not understand sanctification or the interconnection between the two. They understood that forgiveness was all of grace and that their baptism was expressive of their new life in Christ, but they did not understand that their reconciled relationship with God entailed the destruction of sin in their hearts and lives. They did not seem to know that the God who speaks the word of new life in the risen Christ speaks the words of death to the old life in the Old Adam.

So, in response to the question, "What shall we say then?" Paul talks about our relationship with God on deeper and more inward levels than before. This seems especially clear in the emergence of a new kind of vocabulary of sin.

● Spiritual Death and Life

Paul has written in clear and almost terrible language about the sins of the Gentile world and about the sins of the Jews. He has made it plain that "all have sinned and fall short of the glory of God"; and since that is so, we can only be "justified by his grace as a gift" (3:23, 24). In this part of Romans, Paul writes again of sin, but with different language. Look at these new phrases: "our old self," "sinful body," "enslaved to sin," "dead to sin," "slaves of sin" (6:6, 11, 17, 20); "I am carnal, sold under sin," "sin which dwells within me," "law of sin" (7:14, 17, 20, 25); "law of sin and death" (8:2).

Obviously, sin is more than the sum total of the wrong things we have done. In Romans 6, the apostle is talking about a tenacious, persistent ego-centeredness that is as old as Adam and as deep as the wellsprings of life itself. In Romans 1, Paul describes the basic sin of mankind as the unwillingness to let God be God: "For although they knew God they did not honor him as God or give thanks to him" (v. 21). There he reveals mankind's will to autonomy, the desire for self-sovereignty so expressive of our fallen human condition. It is the essence of the carnal mind. In Romans 6, Paul teaches us that this fundamental self-will perseveres in the inner life of the believer. This spirit of self-direction is stubbornly persistent. I believe it can be decisively dealt with only at the cross.

This endemic self-centeredness is understood by anyone who thinks deeply about the human situation. Long ago I memorized these lines from Tagore, a poet from India:

> I come out alone on my way to my tryst
> And who is this that follows me in the silent dark?
> I move aside to escape his company
> But I escape him not.
> He makes the dust rise from the earth with his swagger,
> He adds his loud voice to every word I utter.
> He is my own little self, my Lord.
> He knows no shame.
> But I am ashamed to come into thy presence
> In his company.

Oh, I understand that! "My own little self, my Lord." Someone said, "Everywhere I go, I go too, and that spoils it all." One time my wife and I went to hear Dr. Paul Tournier, Swiss doctor and counselor. We had read his books and had been immensely helped by his insights. He told a story I will never forget. One of his patients had a dream. She and Dr. Tournier were walking down the corridor of a hospital. Both were well dressed, as if to go to church. As they walked, he looked over and saw that protruding from the side of her head was a large nail. She knew she had it. She had done her hair to cover it. She wanted no one to see it. It was her nail. She knew she had it and she knew it had to come out, but she didn't want him to touch it, for she knew that somehow *it was connected to her vital life.*

After telling this story, Dr. Tournier paused and said, "Everyone has a nail."

What is wrong with us—the great anomaly of our life—is not something imposed upon us from the outside. It is somehow connected to our vital life! It is not something we do, but something we are.

Romans 6 describes the problem as "our old self." Albert Edward Day has written that old self does not disappear like an illusion when the facts are known. It has a vitality of its own and has set up connections with the needs and yearnings of the permanent self.

A. W. Tozer has written about the same thing, using the biblical imagery of the "veil on the heart." He says it is the veil of our fleshly, fallen nature—living on within us, unjudged, unrepudiated, uncrucified. It is the closely woven veil of the self life that we have never truly acknowledged, the life of which we are secretly ashamed, and which we have never brought to the cross. The closely woven threads of this veil are the hyphenated sins of the fallen human spirit: self-love, self-pity, self-confidence, self-indulgence, self-righteousness, and a host of others like them. They are the sins of the spirit. They are the sins that produce the egotism, the self-promotion, the exibitionism, and the self-aggrandizement so strangely at home among us. These all are expressions of the "flesh," the fundamental will to autonomy, the self-sovereignty exposed in Romans 1.

Well, what is Paul's answer? What is to be done about the old-self life? Romans 6 makes it plain: In the light of the death of Jesus on the cross and your baptism into him, "consider yourselves dead to sin and alive to God in Christ Jesus" (v. 11). As those who have been brought from death to life, "yield yourselves to God" (v. 13).

The answer is both plain and radical: *Go to the cross with Jesus and die.* Those words are easy to write. They are not easy to obey.

Paul makes it clear that, as we shared in the old life of Adam in our sinful past, we now have died to that life. The dominion of that old way of life has been broken in our death and burial with Christ. We must now identify with his death in the act of considering—"reckoning"—ourselves indeed dead to sin and alive to God. In one sense, we have all died with Christ, of which baptism is a profound symbol. Yet in another sense, that death and that resurrection are brought to living reality in our lives by our "reckoning" of ourselves "dead to sin and alive to God in Christ Jesus" (6:11).

Paul's vivid imagery of death, crucifixion, burial, and resurrection in Romans 6 suggests to me that he is thinking of sin in terms of the fundamental will toward self-direction so characteristic of the Old Adam in us all. Albert E. Day reminds us that the old self does not move off the scene like an actor who gracefully bows and disappears behind the curtain. It is more like an impostor who has usurped God's throne and must be condemned and hanged.

The same idea is differently expressed in the illustration Everett Cattell uses in one of his books: If you put some steel filings on a sheet of paper and pass a magnet beneath it, the filings will form two patterns, one around each pole of the magnet. If ever the filings are to become one harmonious pattern, one of the old patterns must cease. One of the underlying powers must be withdrawn. If ever oneness and harmony are to find expression through our lives, the magnetic pole of self must lose its power.

What I learn from Romans 6 is this: *There is a death to be died before we are dead, so that we may experience a resurrection before we are resurrected.*

• A Strange Kind of Death

The question is, What does it mean to die? When we go to the cross to die with Jesus, what kind of death is it? I believe it does not mean the death of the essential self. The ego itself never dies—that is precisely what lives. Ego is not something I have; it is what I am. I will never die because, in the words of the Westminster Confession, I was meant "to glorify God and enjoy him forever."

Nor does the gospel speak of self-annihilation in the sense of absorption into the All that is God, or Being, or Mind, or Universal Spirit, or Nirvana, or whatever. Nor do I believe that the indwelling Christ replaces my ego or my self; I do not believe that he becomes my inner mind so that I have no separate, discrete selfhood.

Paul says, "It is no longer I who live, but Christ who lives in me." Yet he goes on to say, "The life I now live in the flesh I live by faith" (Gal. 2:20). No, the death we are to die is not the death of the essential self, which was made for fellowship with God. It is the false self that must die. The self that is centered in itself, the pattern of self-centeredness and self-sovereignty, must be brought to the cross and identified with him in death.

I heard the story of an alcoholic who struggled over long years to overcome his problem. He would get his life together, get his wife and family together, and do all right for a while. Then some crisis would get him down again. He would get up, sober up, promise up, and try to live "straight" for a while. Then he would hit the bottom again. Through it all, he had a faithful pastor who loved him and would help and pray for him. Finally, it seemed that he was going to make it. His job, his life, his wife, his family—all were together. Then, late one night, he struggled into his pastor's study. He cried, "Oh, Pastor, if I don't have a drink, I'll die!"

The poor, tired, discouraged pastor looked him full in the face and said, "All right, then. Go home and die!"

And he did. He went home, and he died. On the morrow, a new and different person came to the pastor's study. The old man had died. His real self had not died; it was rather his false, fugitive self that had been unable to face reality and had sought escape in the stupor of drink.

That story does not tell us much about the causes and cures of alcoholism. But it does tell us something about the kind of death we are to die if anything new and different is to come out of our old, dead selves.

What happens to a person who says, "I have to have a drink or I will die"—but who, instead of having a drink, brings all the failures and defenses and insecurities and angers and habits to the cross of Jesus and lets them die with him? I don't believe in magic; but I do believe a real kind of dying takes place in such a situation, which makes new life possible.

What happens to a person who says, "I have to have my way or I'll just die"—but who, instead of exploding in a fit of rage, takes the willfulness and fear and insecurity to the cross and with Jesus says, "Not my will, but thine be done"? That is a real form of dying.

I remember a tall, highly intelligent student who through his college years was very close to our family. He was incredibly bright—and he knew it. He had a fine mind and spoke of it as though it were something separate from himself, which he could train and develop and use to do some great thing for God. But he had a lot of self-will. I have the vivid memory of coming home one night to see him (six feet two inches tall) and my wife, Mary Jo (five feet two inches tall), in a heated discussion, gesturing boldly. He was shouting, "Don't I have a right to do what I want with my life?"

Mary Jo looked up, solemnly shook her head, and said, "No!"

It is one thing to want to do some great thing for God, to desire some great achievement to offer him. It is quite another to surrender ourselves to him so that he can do with us what he wants. That is like dying. It is a dying we all must experience if ever we would know the resurrection life of Jesus.

• The Cross—God's Answer to Sin

Let's go back to Romans 6. Whatever else it is, the cross is God's great No to sin. God's repudiation of sin is expressed in its depth at the cross of Jesus. But the cross is not just something "out there," something that was done for me. It is something in which I must *personally participate*. I must accept to myself the judgment that God rendered on sin there at Calvary and let God say No to sin in me. I must let the cross come into my self-sovereignty, my egotism, my self-centeredness, and my self-preoccupation to say its great *No*. Jesus has not only died for us; he has died *in our place*. So the sentence that God executed upon him we must allow to be executed upon us.

In Emil Brunner's phrase, "We surrender ourselves into his death." By this surrender, we accept God's judgment on sin as a judgment on us. Brunner says that, as one finally says farewell at the grave of a person who lies there below, so we take leave of the old man when we surrender ourselves to die with Christ. Only at the cross can the endless cycle of our self-centeredness be radically disrupted; only there can our false self be exposed and be made real. Only at the cross can the "nail" be removed or the "veil" be torn away. I have read that the peace of God that passes understanding lies on the far side of a cross, on which our sick and disordered selves have submitted to radical surgery and re-creation.

But as the cross is God's No to sin, so the resurrection is God's great Yes to his Son. So it is not really death that we are talking about, but life—resurrection life. There may be a kind of life without death; but resurrection life is possible only on the far side of death. And resurrection life is what we are called to share. We are called to die to the old, destructive, parasitic self that will destroy us if it is not destroyed. God's love in us is toward life; therefore it is destructive of all that would erode or erase the life we have in him. God's Yes in the resurrection becomes our Yes for triumphant living. "All the promises of God find their Yes in him" (2 Cor. 1:20). "For if we have been united with him in a death like his, we shall certainly be united with him in a resurrection like his" (Rom. 6:5).

Samuel Rutherford said that the cross is "such a burden as wings are to a bird or sails are to a boat." The death to which we are called is not a death for destruction, but a death for life. It is not the destruction of the essential person or the essential personhood that is required, but the destruction of the false, self-deceptive self that is centered in itself. Thomas Merton says that in our falseness, we do not even know our true selves until we die. God calls us to reality and life. He seeks to rid us of inward self-dominion and open us to the life-giving dominion of the Spirit of the risen Christ.

● Really Dead . . . and Really Alive!

What keeps all this from becoming a matter of fine words for us Christians who, after all, are not all aglow with holy radiance as we live our ordinary lives in this world? Romans 6 begins with a response to the question, "Are we to continue in sin?" Well, are we?

We are told that we were buried with Christ in baptism and risen with him to new life. We are exhorted to consider ourselves, then, to be dead to sin and alive to God in Christ Jesus. Our old self is crucified; our body of sin is destroyed; our resurrection is experienced. But is this all just an inner mystical experience? Is it merely a playing with words, with no real connection to the way life is really lived?

Some great realities keep Paul's words from being just words. The death of Christ is real. The resurrection of Christ is real. The Holy Spirit is real. Paul has already taught us that faith is not just believing something to be true; it is a personal commitment to Christ as God's Son our Savior, crucified and risen for our salvation. It is our personal response to the personal God who encounters us in Christ through his Spirit.

I see in Romans 6 a resurrection life that is both present and future—at the same time. Our death with Christ is real now, in the sense that we surrender our old selves to his death and begin to live, not in and for ourselves, but for him. Our mortal bodies, through which sin seems to dominate us, will in fact decay and die. But the death we die in Christ before our mortal death is our promise of life in Christ, who never dies.

Our resurrection now with Christ means new freedom and new power in this present life; but it does not nullify our weakness and our human frailty. Our risen life in Christ is both a present reality and a future hope. We live in the tension of the "already" resurrection and the "not yet" consummation of it. So our bodies are still mortal, our earthly lives still subject to temptation and failure. But because we have died with Christ, we live in him; and as certain as his resurrection is our own hope of final glory. I found this translation of an old Greek Christian hymn:

> My God, shall sin its power maintain,
>   And in my soul defiant live?
> 'Tis not enough that Thou forgive;
>   The cross must rise and self be slain.
>
> O God of love, Thy power disclose;
>   'Tis not enough that Christ should rise.
> I, too, must seek the brightening skies
>   And rise from death, as Christ arose.

Karl Barth, in his commentary on Romans, quotes another scholar who says: "With Christ thou art dead unto sin, be then now dead! With Christ thou art risen to life for God, then live now for him! Thou art set at liberty, then now be free!" Our dying is not our own doing, and our living is not our own striving. We have not traded grace for spiritual efforts; nor have we substituted faith for works. We are not saved by grace and then sanctified by struggle. "For *God is at work in you,* both to will and to work for his good pleasure" (Phil. 2:13, italics mine).

● Discussion Questions

1. I did not write about Paul's discussion of Christ and Adam. How would you summarize it (5:12–21)? Are we one in Christ the same way we are one in Adam? Discuss.

2. Why is it that when Paul—or anyone else, for that matter—talks about full, free, and undeserved forgiveness, someone always says that it is too cheap and it makes it too easy to keep sinning?

3. From your point of view, how is Paul's description of sin in chapters 1–3 different from how he talks of it here?

4. I understand from Romans 6 that our fundamental self-centeredness is not automatically broken when we experience justification by faith. Discuss this statement. Do you agree with the connection I have made between the self-sovereignty I find in Romans 1 and the "old self" of chapter 6?

5. Discuss the statement "there is a death to be died before we are dead so that we may live a resurrection life before the resurrection."

6. I have talked about what it means to die with Christ on the basis of my present understanding of Romans. From your understanding, what would you say about it? What other illustrations can you suggest?

7. In summary, how would you answer the question, "Are we to continue in sin that grace may abound?"

CHAPTER · 6

Yielding to Christ

Let not sin therefore reign in your mortal bodies, to make you obey their passions. Do not yield your members to sin as instruments of wickedness, but yield yourselves to God as men who have been brought from death to life, and your members to God as instruments of righteousness. For sin will have no dominion over you, since you are not under law but under grace.

What then? Are we to sin because we are not under law but under grace? By no means! Do you not know that if you yield yourselves to any one as obedient slaves, you are slaves of the one whom you obey, either of sin, which leads to death, or of obedience, which leads to righteousness? But thanks be to God, that you who were once slaves of sin have become obedient from the heart to the standard of teaching to which you were committed, and, having been set free from sin, have become slaves of righteousness. I am speaking in human terms, because of your natural limitations. For just as you once yielded your members to impurity and to greater and greater iniquity, so now yield your members to righteousness for sanctification (Rom. 6:12–19).

● We have regarded the kind of death we are to die with Christ so that we might share in resurrection life with him. We have seen that there is a death to be died—not the death of the real self, but a death of the false, self-centered self; a death to the pattern of self-sovereignty; a death to our fundamental will to autonomy. We know that this death is more than a sentimental desire to do God's will, even though that desire is expressed with fervency and with tears. Christian discipleship means a death to our own self-possession, which is possible only in radical identification with the death of Jesus. This death, we learn in Romans 6, is not something separate from resurrection. As there is a death to be died, so also there is a life to be lived. To die with Jesus means to be raised with him to new life here and now. That new life carries the assurance of resurrection with him at the Last Day.

In the last part of Romans 6, Paul reiterates this theme but with a different emphasis. The word that impresses us in this passage is *yield:* "Do not yield . . . yield yourselves . . . if you yield . . . you once yielded . . . so now yield" (vv. 13, 16, 19). In the light of the cross of Jesus Paul says, "Yield yourself to God as men who have been brought from death to life, and your members to God as instruments of righteousness" (v. 13). The theme of dying/rising moves to the theme of yielding/obeying. It is clear that God calls us to yield ourselves to him.

I do not know how the word *yield* sounds in your ears. Perhaps it is not a good word for you. It may speak of submissive weakness or passive subservience in the presence of wrongful dominance, injustice, or inequality. It may suggest what you have to do when you cannot endure the arm twisting any longer.

It has finally become a very good word for me in my own efforts to understand and live the Christian life. I have come to realize that as we who have been justified by God's grace are led to the cross to die and be raised with Christ, so we are led by his Spirit to live in continuing yieldedness to him. Life in the Spirit or the sanctified life is, I believe, life lived at the Cross in the power of the Resurrection. In the earthly life of Jesus these two were sequential; one followed the other. After the Cross came the Resurrection. But in our lives they are simultaneous; they are experienced together. We do not simply go to the cross with Jesus and then live ever afterward in resurrection power, with no more cross and no more dying in our lives. The Cross is never "behind" us; it is always present in our experience of resurrection power. We live in resurrection power, to be sure; but that power can be released only at the cross, where we are identified with Jesus in his weakness, his obedience, and his death.

It is in this connection that the word *yield* has become instructive for me. It is, incidentally, the word that in Romans 12:1 is translated *present*. Dying is like yielding and yielding is like dying, except that yielding takes the dying "moment" and interprets it as a lifelong process. In Romans 6 it is clear that Paul understood dying and rising with Christ as both past and present experiences. We have died with him and are yet to die with him; we have been raised with him and are yet to live resurrection life in him. So it is with yielding. We are called, in the light of Jesus' death on the cross, to yield ourselves to God in an act of presentation or giving over, and we are to yield ourselves to him in a lifelong process of obedience.

I want to take these ideas of dying/rising and yielding/obeying, put them into the phrase "yield yourselves to God," and relate them to the Spirit's ongoing work of sanctification in our lives. I will do this by discussing some of the ways the word *yield* has become helpful to me.

● Obedience vs. "Good Works"

Perhaps we should be reminded here that our yielding to God is not a subtle form of works. It is the gospel response. We are not justified by faith and sanctified by yielding. We are not saved by grace and sanctified by consecration and moral development. We do not yield ourselves to God so that he will respond to us. We are simply called to respond to his gracious work in Christ. All our Christian experience is of grace through faith. Both our dying and our yielding are dimensions of the faith response of our total selves to the initiative of God.

Yield is a word that helps me understand how I can be who God wants me to be, even when I realize that I cannot actually do what I need to do. For instance, I know that the Holy Spirit calls me to totally consecrate my life to God. I am called to give everything to him—my past, my present, my future—all that I ever have or do or will be. The whole of it is to be yielded to him. I must say that is my intention; that is my whole desire. But I'm not sure I can actually do it. I can want to do it. I can try to do it. I have tried and do try. But is it ever enough? Have I actually given all to him? I'm sure I have—haven't I? I'm positive that I have surrendered everything to him—I think. Right here the word *yield* helps me. I cannot make a *complete* consecration; I cannot make a *total* surrender. All I can do, finally, is yield to God my inability to yield myself to God, in the assurance that I am yielding myself to the one whose Son has made the complete consecration I can never make. Christ has perfectly offered himself—an offering I can never duplicate. So I yield myself to him who has totally yielded himself to his Father.

Long ago I heard preachers speak of the "unknown bundle" we place on the altar of God as part of our placing ourselves there. It is the bundle of all the unknowns about ourselves, about others, and about our future. It is a very good phrase, for that bundle is surely far larger than any "known bundle" we may surrender to him. For me, part of that unknown bundle is my inability to make a truly complete consecration of myself to the Lord. To place it on the altar is to yield to him my inability; it is to present to him my inadequacy; it is to say, "Nothing in my hands I bring; / Simply to Thy cross I cling." It is this yielding, presenting, or letting go that keeps the Christian life from being a continual effort to be better, do better, surrender better, and consecrate more. It is this yielding that releases me from the futile self-efforts to offer God the sacrifice of my total consecration. I am his, and this surrender includes all I can do and all I cannot. As Fénelon would say, I must "let God act."

● **"God Talk" vs. "Good Talk"**

There is a second way the word *yield* helps me. I believe God calls me to be totally sincere. Am I? Of course I am! There is in my heart sincerity "as far as the eye can see." Except the eye cannot really see very far.

I remember talking with a college senior a few days before graduation, who said, "I'm scared. I want to be sincere, but all through college I have been a kidder and have fooled myself. Now I don't know if I am being truthful or if I am still deceiving myself. What if I think I am sincere but am actually self-deluded? How do I know which is which?" Those are *very* hard questions. I only know that we can yield our self-deceptions and our falseness to Christ at the cross. We can say, "Lord, if I am fooling myself, my 'fooling-myself self' is here in your presence. If I am insincere, I am, in my insincerity, sincerely wanting to be in your presence, yielding my self-deceptions and falseness. I yield to you my final inability to truly assess my own motives. I open my closedness to you." In such a prayer, the word *yield* becomes beautiful, for it turns us away from ourselves and turns us to the only One who was himself totally genuine and who alone can discern the thoughts and intents of our hearts.

Earl Lee, who was for years my pastor, used to have us put out our hands and then turn them palms down when we prayed together in worship. It symbolized letting go, releasing into the love of Christ what we had been holding. That may be a good mental picture for those of us who need to release our own self-delusions and self-deceptions and unrealities. Finally, we are not our own judges, even of our own motives. In God only is there "no darkness at all" (1 John 1:5). To the Corinthians, Paul wrote, "I do not even judge myself. . . . It is the Lord who judges me" (1 Cor. 4:3–4). This may be a good time to release our preoccupations with ourselves and our motives, even our examinations of our sincerity, and yield our whole selves to God.

● Self-Understanding vs. Self-Centeredness

Again, the word *yield* helps me when something comes along to remind me that I do not know myself very well. All of us are perplexed by the effort to understand ourselves. In his book *Christian Holiness,* Stephen Neill reminds us of the astonishing depth of human nature. He notes that all great literature, including the Bible, reveals the profound complexity of the human personality. Elizabeth O'Connor has even titled one of her perceptive books *Our Many Selves*.

Elsewhere I have read of "flat characters" and "round characters." These terms refer, not to body shapes, but to character types. "Flat characters" are not changed by the things that happen to them. Cartoon characters, private eyes, and sitcom characters have all kinds of things happen to them, but nothing ever seems to happen in them. They go through weekly adventures fraught with danger, terror, and romance; but they remain unchanged. "Round characters" are those to whom things happen, but *in whom* things happen as well. I think the longtime loyalties generated by such television programs as "Star Trek" and "M.A.S.H." illustrate the appeal of characters whose experiences project self-discovery and who portray real inward change.

It has been years since my twenty-fifth high-school class reunion. Some of the old classmates were just the same—same jokes, same style, same conversations, nothing new. Apparently nothing they experienced in the post-high-school years had produced any intellectual or moral development. Others reflected continued insight and discovery, both of themselves and of the wider world. Some had changed to a remarkable—and unexpected—degree.

One thing is sure: An individual is not just one kind of personality. I sometimes think we have as many layers as an onion. In this context, the ideas of dying/rising and yielding/obeying are especially significant to me.

As I yield myself to God through the processes of self-discovery, the Holy Spirit probes and increasingly reveals my true self. The questions I ask the Holy Spirit are not in vain: Who am I? Why do I act this way? How can it be that I struggle at this time of my life with these temptations? What of my self needs to be revealed to me? Why am I feeling this way? What are the needs in me that prompt the kind of behavior I am manifesting? The illuminating Spirit both prompts and responds to such honest selfprobings. Pondering questions like these, keeping a journal, talking openly and honestly with a trusted friend or counselor, reading the Scripture with an open and prayerful heart—these are the kinds of things the Spirit uses to help me better understand myself.

It is the work of the Spirit to lead us to our true selves in God. He would guide us to the real self that, as Thomas Merton said, we never know until we die. We can never come of maturity without yielding our experiences of self-insight and discovery to God.

It is wonderful that I can yield to God the things I discover about myself, in the confidence that his revealing Spirit is the cleansing Spirit. This is especially wonderful in the light of the fact that I learned the good and great things about myself long ago, and what I have been learning lately is all that other stuff!

Once, when she was about ten, my daughter needed to be disciplined. Right in the middle of punishing her, I suddenly realized that I was my father. It wasn't that I was acting like my father—I *was* he. I never have been the same. Suddenly, I understood myself—and my father—more profoundly than ever before. It was an experience both good and bad. I realized where a lot of my feelings and attitudes had come from—some of which I was not especially proud. But in my new awareness I had a new freedom and a new hope. As I reflected on those insights in the presence of God, I was enabled to yield to him parts of myself I had not clearly understood before. And in the yielding there was healing.

That experience is a good example of the way the Spirit works to bring us to insight, and so to change. There have been a hundred other times like that in my life—mostly painful, I confess—through which the Holy Spirit has revealed attitudes, desires, and fears I never even knew I had. Yielding these new self-discoveries to God does not produce instant change like magic. However, I believe that if new insights are to produce any inner transformation and growth toward maturity, it will take more than my own ability to accept them and try to integrate them into my life. I need the cleansing and healing work of the Spirit. I need a place to go when I realize that I do not know myself very well. I need a place to bring my unknowings and false self-perceptions. I need a place of genuine renewal, a source of new beginning for my old and disillusioned self. There is such a place. It is the cross of Jesus where I may go and die with him, there to share the new life of his resurrection.

No, I don't need a place to go—I need a Person to come to me, a Person who can lead me through my own dying and rising, who can lead me to the true self I could never discover alone. Such a Person has come. I may yield my knowing, unknowing, growing self to him.

• Change vs. Stability

We could speak of many things, for there is no dimension of our lives that may not be yielded to the revealing and healing presence of God. But I should like to close this chapter with one further way the word *yield* has been especially helpful to me.

I am reminded of a point made in Stephen Neill's book referred to earlier. He writes that we should not think of human life as though it were permanent or static; yet, in spite of all our efforts to the contrary, we think of our personal relationships in those very categories. We assume that things and people aren't supposed to change. Even though we know better, even though we ourselves seek to be agents of productive change, we don't want things to change.

This is not the place to discuss the source of our hunger for permanence underneath our restless pursuit of change. I think it is somehow of God. But the truth is, life *does* change and I must yield to that.

I vividly remember a moment of vision when my daughter Susan was about eleven. I saw her coming down the block, on her way home from school. She was walking and then, seeing me, running to meet me. For the first time, I desperately wanted to hold back the calendar and stop the clock. That moment seemed to symbolize all the goodness of our lives. We had home and work and family and love. And for all the imperfections, I really liked things the way they were. Since their births we had hurried the children on—out of diapers, into school, on toward adulthood. But on that day I silently cried "No!" to the inexorable process. It was a most ineffectual no. What does one do at such a time?

That was more than twenty years ago. What of all that has happened to us all in those fleeting years? They have been years of goodness and beauty, of darkness and sorrow, of hurt and healing, of sickness and health—and growing older. Everything is changing and there is no going back. I recall the old lines from Omar Khayyam:

> The Moving Finger writes, and, having writ,
> Moves on; nor all your Piety nor Wit
> Shall lure it back to cancel half a line,
> Nor all your Tears wash out a Word of it.

True, and no help to me at all! I also remember the lines of Henry Lyte in "Abide With Me":

> Change and decay in all around I see,
> Oh, Thou who changest not, abide with me.

Now that is what makes yielding to God such a beautiful thing!

> Hearken to me, O house of Jacob,
>   all the remnant of the house of Israel,
>   who have been borne by me from your birth,
>   carried from the womb;
>   even to your old age I am He,
>   and to gray hairs I will carry you.
>   I have made, and I will bear;
>   I will carry and will save (Isa. 46:3–4).

The clear command is also a gracious promise: "Yield yourselves to God." Into his care we may surrender the changing times and seasons of our lives. If there is no continual yielding or surrendering to God, we are bound to the endless passage of the years, slaves to the irrevocable process of decay. We are locked to the descending spiral of inability and unknowing and self-deception.

We are unwitting victims of the destructive cycle of "greater and greater iniquity" (Rom. 6:19). That cycle has been operating for a long, long time in our fallen and falling world. But it is not the last reality. It is not the inevitable truth.

The good phrase, "yield yourselves to God," is both a command and an enabling promise. There is freedom for a new kind of future when we relinquish to God our old selves, with our old habitual and destructive loyalties. We may then receive the promise of his new future. "Now that you have been set free from sin and have become slaves of God, the return you get is sanctification and its end, eternal life" (Rom. 6:22).

● **Discussion Questions**

1. I have talked about yielding in terms of its connection with dying. In your mind how are they connected? How are they different?
2. Is the word *yield* helpful to you? What other terms are found in the Bible versions you have? What other terms would you use? Why?
3. Discuss the statement "both our dying and our yielding are dimensions of the faith response of our total selves to the initiative of God."
4. How do we keep our yielding or surrendering to God from becoming a refined form of works?
5. In addition to the ways mentioned, what are some ways you have learned to know yourself? Have you ever had the experience of "being" your father or mother in a way that has made you suddenly understand yourself in a new way? Explain.

CHAPTER · 7

Jesus Means Freedom

Do you not know, brethren—for I am speaking to those who know the law—that the law is binding on a person only during his life? Thus a married woman is bound by law to her husband as long as he lives; but if her husband dies she is discharged from the law concerning the husband. . . .

Likewise, my brethren, you have died to the law through the body of Christ, so that you may belong to another, to him who has been raised from the dead in order that we may bear fruit for God. While we were living in the flesh, our sinful passions, aroused by the law, were at work in our members to bear fruit for death. But now we are discharged from the law, dead to that which held us captive, so that we serve not under the old written code but in the new life of the Spirit (Rom. 7:1–2, 4–6).

● We have viewed Romans 6 from the perspective of freedom from the tyranny of the old-self life as we die and rise with Christ, and the perspective of the growth we experience as we continue to yield ourselves to God. In the first part of Romans 7 we learn of another dimension of freedom. It is freedom from legalism. Paul writes, "You have died to the law through the body of Christ. . . . discharged from the law, . . . so that we serve not under the old written code but in the new life of the Spirit" (7:4, 6).

I used to think legalism was generally a pretty dead issue among Christians. I do not think so any more. I have come to realize that we still seek to salve our consciences with our decent behavior and general morality. We have been faithful in performance of duty;

we have reminded ourselves constantly that we have done our best, or at least as well as others would have done in our place. We certainly are not as bad as many, and are probably better than most. We know we are not perfect, but we are glad that we haven't actually done badly. At least we are not hypocrites!

This is precisely the kind of legalistic thinking from which Christ would set us free. By *legalism* I mean the bondage of external conformity to moral law as a means of expressing our right relationship with God. The term covers all kinds of conformity patterns—overt, covert, blatant, subtle, written, oral—all attempts to meet common religious expectations. Actually, I am talking about the tendency of all human behavior patterns to stifle, to bind, and to control, and how these habits lead to complacency or pride or guilt or judgment. I am concerned how these behavior patterns take the place of a genuine personal relationship with God in Christ.

The Christian life is not a moral struggle to obey some set of externalized commands in rote fashion. It is the spiritual struggle to remain open to the creative leading of the Spirit of Christ. But, for too many, the Christian life is precisely that kind of moral struggle to meet other people's expectations.

• The Journey From Slavery to Bondage

Paul certainly knew about legalism and its moral struggles. He was a Pharisee of the Pharisees, blue blood of the blue bloods, blameless under the law, and zealous in persecuting the church (Phil. 3:5–6). And it all left him with despair, not with freedom. None of his efforts could free him from the "goads" (Acts 26:14). He was brought up in the religious system and pursued it all the way with all his heart, but he never found freedom until he met Jesus. Paul knew about legalism, all right.

The Jews were not always bound by legalism. Remember the Exodus story? Down in the land of Egypt, where the great god-incarnate Pharaoh ruled, the poor folk were slaving in the brickyards and crying out to God the pain of their injustice. And the Lord listened. Remember how he appeared to Moses on the back slopes of Mount Horeb and said to him in the burning bush, "I have seen the afflication of my people . . . and have heard their cry . . . I know their sufferings, and I have come down to deliver them" (Exod. 3:7–8)? With mighty signs and wonders, the God who is true God brought down the gods who were no gods and set his rag-tag nobodies free. He brought them across the sea, preserved them through the wilderness, and led them to Sinai. He said to them, in effect, "I have created you. I have redeemed you. I have delivered you. Now, will you belong to me?"

The Israelites said, "Yes, we will."

So there at Sinai, God and his people entered into a covenant relationship expressed in the marvelous formula: "I will be your God, and you will be my people."

That relationship, based on redeeming love, was lived out in two primary ways. First, it was expressed through the Hebrew rituals and ceremonies, the holy times and seasons. Their sacrifices, offerings, worship rituals, their feasts of Passover, Pentecost, and Tabernacles—all these celebrated and renewed their covenant relationship with God who had saved and redeemed them. Second, Israel's relationship was expressed in their daily lifestyle, in behavior expressive of the character of the holy God who had called them to himself. The Torah, the Ten Commandments, and the Book of the Covenant described how they were to live. (The Ten Commandments, you know, were not given to mankind in general—though, as expressive of God's character and will, they are indeed good for all mankind. The Commandments were given to a particular people who had been saved, delivered, and protected by God. In the Old Testament we witness the creation, the deliverance, and the calling of this people. Then came the worship and lifestyle instructions that were given to celebrate and express the joy of covenant relationship.)

I like to think of it this way: After Sinai, Israel walked on into the future with God on the two legs of worship and lifestyle, or ritual and commandment. They did not worship as they did to create a right relationship with God; they did not obey as they did in order to win acceptance with him. They already were his redeemed and covenanted people. Their worship and lifestyle were God-given ways in which they were to express and live out the joyful relationship already established with God in the Exodus and the covenant at Sinai.

Years later, however, another generation arose that had not shared the great primary experiences. They had not come across the Red Sea; they had not been to Sinai with its awesome fire and smoke and glory. For the first generation, the worship-lifestyle system had well expressed their joyous relationship with God. The second generation and those following grew up under the system and did not know the relationship on which it was based. For the first Israelites, the relationship came first; for the later Israelites, the system came first. For these later ones, the relationship with God was supposed to be established as they identified themselves with the faith of their fathers and as they made the promises and demands of the covenant their own.

It is not hard to see how a system that celebrates and expresses a relationship with God can become the supposed means by which that relationship is established and certified. That is essentially what happened when the remnant of Judah came back to their homeland from exile in Babylon. Their holy city, now desolate, was inhabited by people of mixed races and religions. The question of the day was, "Who is a true Israelite?" The clear answer was, "The one who keeps the law." And there you have the seeds of legalism.

What a destructive inversion! The law given to interpret a relationship with God became the means by which the relationship was established and defined.

Paul knew very well about all this. He grew up in it, believing with all his heart that the keeping of the law was the way to be right with God. He honestly tried to do and be all that mainline Pharisaism said he should, and the effort drove him to despair. It was all the worse because he had identified this system with the will of God. No wonder he said, "Wretched man that I am!" (Rom.

7:24). When conformity to the law package (or moral system) becomes the way we try to become right with God, it does not produce life. It produces death. In this sense, law produces death the same way sin produces death. This kind of law keeping throws us back upon our own efforts to achieve a relationship with God. But that relationship can never be earned; it can only be received.

Let me tell a little of my own story. My grandfather was an evangelist known as "Uncle Buddy" Robinson. He was marvelously converted in an old-fashioned brush arbor campmeeting in Dallas County, Texas, in the summer of 1880. He grew up in a place where there were "two rocks for every dirt." They were so poor, he said, that they "ate dried apples for breakfast, drank hot water for lunch, and let them swell for supper." "Uncle Buddy" couldn't read or write much. He stuttered a lot. He owned little more than his horse and saddle, a six-shooter, and a "greasy deck of cards." But he was part of the Holiness Revival that was sweeping through the country. It transformed his whole life. He joined with others who had experienced the cleansing and the power of the Spirit in their lives. That revival experience brought together like-minded groups and persons, some of whom had come out of their old formal churches, others of whom had been "put out" of them. They were drawn together as though by some divine magnet, bound together by the shared experience of the cleansing, empowering presence of the Spirit.

They often met together. They prayed and praised and worshiped together. They talked about how they should live in the world as Spirit-filled people. They talked about how they should worship, how they should govern themselves, what should be their agreed beliefs and their mutually accepted lifestyle. When it was all over, they printed all this in a black-covered book and called it the *Manual*. It came out of a new, joyous experience of the presence of God's Spirit. For my grandfather and those like him, the experience of this revival fellowship produced the worship patterns, the doctrinal expressions, and the lifestyle guidance. Codified, printed, and bound, these expressions became the bases of a denominational ethos or "system."

This is the tradition into which I was born. I'm a third-generation member of my denomination, so I grew up with both the book and the Bible; I met the system before I met the Savior. Much of my own early spiritual journey could be described as the process of sorting out what was system and what was Savior.

I have learned that the sorting is not a simple process. It is not something that, once accomplished, can be left in the past. It is still going on in my life. I wish I knew why it is so hard to keep the two in perspective. I live in the context of a denominational system—I can't help it. That system includes not only my church or denomination or fellowship. It includes the way I have come to think of life and values and religion in general.

None of us lives in a cultural vacuum; no one is free from basic assumptions and perspectives that condition how the gospel is heard, how the Bible is read, or how the Christian life is to be understood. We live in the context of a system at the same time that we live in relationship with the Savior. I suppose there really is no way to separate the two. We cannot come to know Christ in a way uninfluenced by our religious heritage or our cultural environment.

However, if we really listen to Paul, we may understand that our problem is not that there is Torah or moral law or a denominational system or a Western culture. Our real problem is that we do what Israel did. We do what Paul did and what a lot of Christians are still doing. We identify the law—the system—with the relationship we need to have with God. So we turn the whole thing upside down. We begin to think that we become acceptable to God by conforming to the doctrinal or worship or lifestyle patterns of our group. We think we are in right relationship with God when we are in right relationship with the religious structure; or we think that the quality of our relationship with God is determined by the degree to which we conform to the pattern or mores of that structure. This is legalism. And it leads to death.

● The Consequences of Legalism

When we confuse the system with the relationship, we open ourselves to problems from two sides. On one side, those who are by nature conformers or joiners can come into the Christian faith and pick up the patterns with seeming ease. They join up and fit in. They are readily accepted and affirmed and supported in their cooperative behaviors. Perhaps their entrance into the Christian faith is actually entrance into a Christian subculture. They may have simply traded a worldly group structure for a spiritual group structure, without coming to a relationship with Christ in which the whole structure of life is brought under his judgment and grace, and thus under his lordship.

On the other side are those who tend to be noncompliant, who are just naturally antagonistic to structured systems. They react negatively to any laws, rules, and regulations. They are "cut on the bias," as our family used to say. And they are the ones who are not quite so accepted and not quite so affirmed and hardly ever supported in their noncooperative behaviors. Could it be that their rejection of the Christian faith is not actually a rejection of the faith, but a rejection of the system or the subculture that is identified with the Christian faith?

I used to think that the conformers were more likely to be righteous legalists, while the rebels were more likely to be unrighteous unlegalists. But I have come to believe that sometimes the ones who rebel are in fact closet legalists. They are like a lot of us who persist in believing that we must meet demands we know we cannot meet. They say, "I can't live it." Yet they believe that what they cannot live is precisely what God demands of them. So their problem is compounded. They can neither pick up the impossible burden or reject the whole thing. In either case—conformist or rebel—the basic assumption is too often the same: that a real relationship with God is found in identification with some external conformity pattern. One group says yes, the other says no to that pattern. But it is profoundly tragic when our yes or no is said, not to the Savior, but to the system.

Is not this the same sort of painful situation Paul experienced? For all his efforts and struggles, he couldn't keep the very law he believed would make him right with God. He tried, and for that matter did better than anyone else he knew; but it was never enough to bring him to freedom and joy in his God. Yet he couldn't say no to the law; he couldn't reject the system, because he believed it was God's way to righteousness.

While Paul's experience with the law taught him he couldn't keep it, his experience with Christ taught him he didn't have to! When he said yes to God's righteousness in Jesus, he was set free from legalism. He discovered—no, God revealed to him—that his right relationship with God was not based on his efforts to conform to any external code. He was made right with God through faith in God's own gift of himself in Jesus. He was free to "serve not under the old written code but in the new life of the Spirit" (Rom. 7:6). He did not trade one system (external law) for another (internal compulsion). The freedom he found in Christ transformed the basic assumptions of his legalistic spirit. He was unhinged from his basic belief that he had to earn his way with God. Dying with Christ meant the death of every self-effort toward salvation, even the self-effort to keep the law of God!

Christ would set us free from this basic assumption of the legalistic spirit. Christ in his death destroys our false, tenacious conviction that we must earn our way with God. Can we ever believe it? Will we ever receive it?

Jesus means freedom from bondage to external conformity as a means of producing righteousness. He would free us from our self-struggles to be his children. "We are discharged from the law, dead to that which held us captive, so that we serve not under the old written code but in the new life of the Spirit" (Rom. 7:6). I wish it were as simple to grasp the truth and believe the freedom as it is to put the words together. But even after we find in Christ this freedom from legalism, the longest and most difficult task we have is to keep it! The Christian life is not the moral struggle to obey a set of commands in rote fashion. But it does involve an authentic and constructive struggle: the struggle to keep open to the creative leading of the Spirit of Christ and not "submit again to a yoke of slavery" (Gal. 5:1).

We are not set free from the moral law or the denominational system or the Christian subculture. These are never eliminated in the Christian fellowship. The law cannot be abrogated; the culture and system cannot be denied. What is abrogated is our dependency upon them to make us right with God; what is denied is their role in bringing us into the body of Christ. We are free, then, to live in the fellowship of our particular group or denomination as part of the body of Christ. We are free to function within a religious system. We are free in the Spirit to serve Christ. We are bound in Christian love to be faithful to the disciplines, loyal to the fellowship, and true to the aims of our church group or denomination. But freedom in Christ enables us to keep those disciplines without being oppressed by them. Our liberty in his love keeps our fellowship open and nonconstrictive. We may pursue the goals of our church without being manipulated by them because we have been released to serve, "not under the old written code but in the new life of the Spirit" (Rom. 7:6).

A personal encounter illuminated this problem of legalism for me. A student, soon to graduate, said to me, "You know, I never have really given my heart to Christ because I know that, if I did, he would want me to be a preacher. And I don't want to be that."

We talked a long while, and finally I said, "You are going to live your whole life running from God because you think he wants you to preach. What if you get to the end of your miserable existence and the Lord says to you, 'Dave, all your mother's prayers couldn't convince me to call you to preach. I wouldn't have you as a preacher on a silver platter!'? Maybe what he wants is just you, with your heart open to him in freedom and love."

The spirit of legalism was killing my friend. He wasn't rejecting the Savior; he was rejecting the false assumption that to be God's man he had to do precisely what he knew he could not do. In his case, though, that move entailed rejection of the Savior.

Well, I hope I was ultimately helpful in my talk with Dave. I know the encounter was very helpful to me. Through it I understood in a new way both the pervasiveness and the destructiveness of legalism. For Dave, it was not the legalism of rule keeping but of expectation keeping. I saw that Jesus wanted to set him free from false fears and expectations to live a life of service and joy. He wants that for you and me as well. Jesus means freedom from legalism. I love these old lines:

> To run and work, the law commands,
> Yet gives me neither feet nor hands;
> But better news the gospel brings,
> It bids me fly, and gives me wings!

• Discussion Questions

1. How would you define legalism? Do you think I have portrayed legalism in the church as a bigger problem than it really is? Discuss.
2. I have written at length about the way the idea of law changed during the period from Moses to Paul. In your own words, how would you describe this change?
3. How would you describe the difference between my grandfather's conversion and my own?
4. I have said that our real problem is not that there is a moral law or a religious system; rather, the problem is that we think conformity to the law system will lead us into a saving relationship with Christ. Do you agree or disagree with this observation? Discuss.
5. If we are not saved by conformity to some external standard of belief or conduct, how are we "kept on track" ethically?
6. Do you agree that some people who act rebelliously toward God and the church are actually disheartened legalists? How can we help these people find freedom in Christ?
7. List some ways that our freedom in Christ enables us to live within our cultural/religious system and still be free.

CHAPTER · 8

Freedom From the Law of Sin and Death

We know that the law is spiritual; but I am carnal, sold under sin. I do not understand my own actions. For I do not do what I want, but I do the very thing I hate. . . . So then it is no longer I that do it, but sin which dwells within me. . . . I can will what is right, but I cannot do it. . . .

So I find it to be a law that when I want to do right, evil lies close at hand. . . . I see in my members another law at war with the law of my mind and making me captive to the law of sin which dwells in my members. Wretched man that I am! Who will deliver me from this body of death? Thanks be to God through Jesus Christ our Lord! So then, I of myself serve the law of God with my mind, but with my flesh I serve the law of sin. There is therefore now no condemnation for those who are in Christ Jesus. For the law of the Spirit of life in Christ Jesus has set me free from the law of sin and death. For God has done what the law, weakened by the flesh, could not do: sending his own Son in the likeness of sinful flesh and for sin, he condemned sin in the flesh, in order that the just requirement of the law might be fulfilled in us, who walk not according to the flesh but according to the Spirit (Rom. 7:14–15, 17–18, 21, 23–25; 8:1–4).

● In this part of Romans, Paul offers another use of the word *law*. In the first part of Romans 7, *law* refers to the Torah, the Mosaic legal code viewed as a whole, which was understood to describe the life pleasing to God. When Paul writes in Romans 7:1, "I am speaking to those who know the law," he is referring to the law of Moses, the Torah. Understood this way, *law* also stands for those religious conformity patterns and lifestyle demands by which relationship with God is thought to be achieved or approved or certified. The end result of such law is deadening legalism—from which, by his death, Jesus sets us free to live in the Spirit.

The Scripture verses before us at the beginning of this chapter reflect a different use of *law*. In 7:21, Paul says, "I find it to be a law that when I want to do right, evil lies close at hand." In 8:2, he uses the phrase, "law of sin and death." Here the word *law* expresses a principle of power and action. In this case, *law* is not something given out or something received; it is something experienced. In the phrase, "law of sin and death," Paul is using the word much the same way we would use it when speaking of the law of gravity. That law was not passed by the legislature nor does it need to be enforced. It is simply "there," exercising a continuous, powerful influence upon us all.

• The Persistent Power of Sin

The phrase, "law of sin and death," reveals a new and terrible dimension of sin in relation to law. We have seen that in Romans 6 Paul talks of sin in terms of self-sovereignty, sin as an expression of our fundamental will to self-direction or autonomy. Here he talks about sin as a dynamic power that lays hold of persons, making them "captive to the law of sin" (7:23). I believe that we are far more naïve about the power of sin than was the apostle. It is more than self-centeredness and more than self-sovereignty; it is a dynamic force within our lives. We cannot simply add up all the sins of omission and the sins of commission and get the bottom line of sin. We commit sinful acts, to be sure; we have a fatal flaw, without doubt. But sin is more. It is a force with awesome, demonic power.

Paul does not tell us what specific experience of his life awakened him to the reality and power of sin. He may have had some boyhood transgression in mind, or he may have been speaking in personal terms of the experience of guilt common to us all. Every person becomes his own Adam and "falls." Paul may have been thinking of coveteousness, everyone's sin, and of himself as the symbol of everyone.

Clearly, there was a time when he did not know the power of sin in relation to the law or to himself. When the awakening did come, it was not an awakening to life, but to the realization of the power of sin to distort the law and to bring him to death (Rom. 7:7–11).

This is not the place to examine at any length the hard questions that arise in connection with Paul's use of the personal pronoun in Romans 7. Here are some perspectives that are helpful to me:

1. I believe that Paul speaks as a Pharisee who had come up under the Law. Only a thoroughgoing Jew could use the law language he uses and in the way he uses it. He cannot get out of his "law" orientation any more than we can get into it.

2. I believe that Paul also speaks as a human being, a descendant of Adam. He uses the personal pronoun *I,* but in using it he identifies himself with fallen mankind in Adam—and he identifies fallen mankind with himself.

3. I believe that Paul speaks as a Christian. Only a person in Christ can speak so deeply of the will and the law of God and of the inner struggle with sin. Only a person in Christ can probe so truly the inner turmoil of one outside Christ.

In summary, Paul the Jew who knows life under the law, Paul the man who knows himself to be one with fallen mankind in Adam, and Paul the Christian who has experienced the victory of Christ writes with profound understanding of the destructive power of sin. He understands, regardless of his perspective, that sin distorts the God-given purpose of the law and the God-designed purpose of mankind. Let's give careful attention to these two dimensions of the destructive power of sin.

● A Distortion of the Law

Paul learned that sin distorts the God-given purpose of the law. The law was given after the covenant relationship between God and humanity had been established, as a vehicle for celebrating and living out the covenant relationship. It gave answer to the question: How are the people of God to live in the world and be God's people? The law came to be used later as a means for becoming right with God and as a standard for measuring the people of God. It thus became a source of legalism. But is it enough to say that God's good law was used badly and so produced bad results? That is true enough, but Paul's radical language and the intense emotion in Romans 7 tell us there is more. For all its value in preserving the created order, for all its worth in driving sinful people to their need of a Savior, for all the guidance it gives to the Christian, law is the very thing sin uses to destroy a person.

How can this be? First, law defines sin and so "creates" it. My wife, Mary Jo, and I used to play a lot of tennis. There was a great place not far from the parsonage. One day a truck from the recreation department arrived and some men began painting lines on the concrete. The next week they put a net across the space that separated us. That's when all the fun went out of tennis. All we ever did, it seemed, was something wrong. Now we had lines to stay inside of and a net to get the ball over. We figured we had better quit before someone came to tell us we had to keep score. We didn't know our transgressions until the law came; and we haven't played much tennis since! Perhaps what is wrong with tennis is not the rules, but what age and ineptness have done to those who try to play it. Likewise Paul would remind us that the problem is not the law, but what sin has done to those who try to keep it.

Second, law has a seductive way of creating a fascination for what it prohibits. I remember the old story of the mother, nervous about leaving her young children with the sitter and aware of all that could go wrong, who said as she went out the door, "Now remember, don't put any peas up your nose!" There was actually nothing wrong with the advice, but peas suddenly took on a strange and new fascination.

Law itself is neutral. But the prohibition, "Thou shalt not," arouses in the self its "I shall." Something rebellious is awakened in the presence of a prohibition. When law, thus inverted, is master, it has the same effect as though sin were the master. Paul found it so.

And so did Augustine. A. M. Hunter, in his book on Romans, recounts the familiar story of the stormy night Augustine and his young friends raided a neighbor's pear orchard. (Perhaps it was not unlike Paul's own "covet" experience of Rom. 7:7–8.) That experience symbolized for Augustine his ability to know right from wrong—and his moral inability to do the right instead of the wrong. In later years he interpreted the event something like this: "They were nice pears, but it was not the wretched pears my soul coveted, for I had plenty better at home. I picked them simply because I wanted to be a thief. What was it that I wanted in the theft? Was it the pleasure of acting against law in order that I, a prisoner under rules, might have a maimed counterfeit of freedom by doing with impunity what was forbidden, with a dim similitude of omnipotence?"

The language is certainly not contemporary, but Augustine's analysis of the episode is profoundly relevant. What did he want in the theft? If not pears, then why steal? The law was the symbol of constraints upon his life; it was also the source of his desire to disobey. The presence of law lets us know that we are not God. We are not in total freedom. Fallen self would be self-sovereign and cannot stand the presence of restraint upon its supposed omnipotence. The specific thing the law prohibits becomes the thing most necessary to do or to have, because that thing expresses the limitation we cannot tolerate. The tragedy is that the transgression does not bring the fulfillment of a free, self-directed action; it only compounds our guilt. The supposedly autonomous act of freedom is actually the obedient response of a slave-self, bound to its master, sin.

● A Destruction of God's Purpose

Paul also learned how the power of sin works to destroy the God-designed purpose for mankind. A word in 1 John reflects this same understanding of sin. It is *world*: "For all that is in the world, the lust of the flesh and the lust of the eyes and the pride of life, is not of the Father but is of the world" (1 John 2:16).

I understand the word *world* to refer to human society as it structures itself apart from the sovereignty of God. This structure of false values, unrealities, and deceits exercises a molding force over each new life born into it. The dynamic power of sin in the world is a molding force; this is illustrated, for example, by the awesome power of the liquor business. Its power is more than the money spent or the advertisements promoted or the ego needs of the top management. The liquor business is locked into the fallen ego needs of the whole society; it plays upon our insecurities and needs in such a way that an entire culture is built upon it. The sports syndicate, the political system, and elegant society have embraced it—and all the while everyone knows it will destroy us.

Or shall we talk of illicit drugs? The power of the drug traffic is more—much more—than the power hunger of the big drug kings; it is more than the money hunger of their courier slaves; it is more than just the emptiness and the insecurity of bored adults or stressed young professional achievers or weak peer-pressured adolescents. There is a demonic spirit—a weird dynamic of self-destruction that is more pervasive than our accumulated statistics could ever reveal.

Or shall we talk of the entertainment business, the video-punk-rock culture that exercises incredible, unmeasurable influence upon our lives? It is a dark and increasingly obvious demonic power, molding new lives born into society.

Let us not suppose that the power of sin is only exercised blatantly in the world. No sanctuary is immune to the invasion. We know Christians whose whole lives are consumed with trading for a new RV or another boat or house or car. They come alive at the game. Sports is the god before whom all others must finally bow. For some Christians, life really centers on the soft porn of the afternoon soap operas. I sense these days, through the dramatic increase of intense advertising, an almost desperate drive for money and for the lifestyle and the security it promises. There is no need to multiply obvious illustrations of the manifest power of sin among us.

Regardless of how intelligent we may be, how fine or beautiful or talented, regardless of what our wonderful heritage is—if we yield ourselves to the world's influence, it will bring us to destruction. I heard of a man looking out of the tenth-floor window of a fifteen-story hotel. He saw a man falling from an upper floor. Moments later, hearing the sirens and all the commotion, he rushed down to the main lobby, out on to the street, and saw the awful mess. "Strange," he said. "I saw him just a moment ago and he looked fine." At the time the spectator saw him, he was fine. But he was subject to a law; he was in the grip of a force that brought him to destruction.

I wish that were nothing more than a dumb story. But I am thinking of real persons I saw not long ago—and they looked fine. You can think of persons you saw months ago or years ago who looked fine. But they aren't, because they are in the grip of forces that bring inevitable destruction. I wonder if we really believe this. A friend who recently returned to the workplace after some years of absence said to me, "There is a monster out there!" The real problem is that the monster is not just "out there"—it is "in here."

Paul teaches that the power of sin has laid hold of us through the flesh—our unregenerate human nature. We are subject to the influences of our bodily desires and the molding influence of the world and its values. Our weak and fallen embodied selves become slaves of sin. So it is not enough to say, "I've got to get my act together. Give me some time and I can handle my life. I can get free from this involvement. I can break this habit. I can work out my problems." Paul said he had no confidence in the flesh (Phil. 3:3), and I have come to agree with him. Have you?

• We Cannot Master Ourselves

It is hard to let go our self-confidence, our dependency upon the flesh. The dynamic power of sin is greater than we are. No one can be his own moral master. Augustine said, "How oft have I lashed at my will and cried, 'Leap now, leap now!' And I crouched for the leap and all but leaped. But I did not leap. And the life to which I was accustomed held me more than the life for which I really yearned." We can all understand that profound anguish.

Paul cried, "Wretched man that I am! Who will deliver me from this body of death?" The gospel answered with the word of triumph, "Thanks be to God through Jesus Christ our Lord!" (Rom. 7:24–25). Ian Thomas wrote, "I can't. He never said I could. He can! and said He always would."

We are well aware of the awesome power of the law of sin and death. But there is another law, "the law of the Spirit of life in Christ Jesus," and it sets us "free from the law of sin and death" (Rom. 8:2). Christ has entered the realm where sin had claimed jurisdiction, and he has won for us the freedom we may share. What law could not do, God has done. He has sent his Son "in the likeness of sinful flesh and for sin, he condemned sin in the flesh" (Rom. 8:3). The power of sin's dominion cannot be broken by our human efforts. It cannot be broken by the law. But God in Jesus has done it. Coming all the way into our human sinful situation, "in the likeness of sinful flesh," God has "condemned sin in the flesh" (Rom. 8:3). It is this very point that makes the gospel such good news of freedom. Christ has come into the arena of our struggle and has won the victory where we have lost it.

I think we have the mental image of Jesus' winning the victory for us "up there" somewhere or "back there" somewhere. But he wins the victory for us right here!

Where do we lose the battle? In the flesh. The weakness of the flesh is our problem. Remember, *flesh* does not mean just our physical bodies or our sensual desires (though these are, of course, part of our fleshly reality). *Flesh* means human nature on its own, by itself, centered in itself in its fallenness, unable to do what it wants to do by itself. *Flesh* means the unregenerate self in its fallenness, apart from God. In that situation—in the flesh—we cannot win the fight against the power of sin. But Jesus has come into our human nature, right where we are in our weakness and failure, and wins the victory for us.

Where do you struggle? Where do you fight the battle? Where does temptation really tempt you? Can you understand that Jesus wins the victory right where you struggle? He comes to you right where you are hurting, right where you are failing, right where you are unable to prevail, and right there he is your victory.

Jesus can make a real difference. He can set us free. That means we are not locked into our failures. We are not locked into the old destructive habit patterns. We are not destined to keep on struggling the same old struggles, losing the same old battles, carrying the same old problems the rest of our lives. The victory of Jesus is real. It has been won right where we live, and we may share it. There is another law besides the law of sin and death. It is the law of life; it is the law of the Spirit. That law is not something—it is Someone who, by his Spirit, comes to us in our weakness with his strength and "breaks the power of cancelled sin and sets the prisoner free."

● The Futility of Self-Deliverance

Paul makes a curious statement between the victory he declares in Romans 7 and the victory he shares in Romans 8. "Who will deliver me from this body of death? Thanks be to God through Jesus Christ our Lord! So then, I of myself serve the law of God with my mind, but with my flesh I serve the law of sin" (7:24–25). It sounds like a classic anticlimax. In a way, it is—but true.

The key phrase is "I of myself." Who delivers us? Christ our Lord. When "I of myself" am in charge, I experience the hopeless struggle between what I want to do and what I end up doing. I condemn myself to the failing cycle of knowing what is right and not being able to perform it—on one level saying yes to God, on the other saying yes to self. That is always the way it is when I am by myself and of myself.

But we are not of ourselves! "There is . . . no condemnation for those who are in Christ Jesus" (8:1). In Romans 7:17 and 20 the lament is, "No longer I . . . but sin which dwells within me." But in Galatians 2:20 the victory is expressed in the testimony, "I have been crucified with Christ; it is no longer I who live, but Christ who lives in me." On the one hand, the Christian's portrait could be *not I but sin;* on the other, it is *not I but Christ.* He is the one who frees us from the cycle of our defeat.

At a laymen's retreat I was handed a letter written by a woman who was a student years ago in my classes at college. It was a remarkable testimony to the new freedom she had found in Christ. She had been bound to the habits of liquor and drugs. She wrote of bondage to lust, to sexual fantasies, and to relationships that were destructive. She had been abused as a child and hated her mother who said she didn't want her to be born. It read like a case study in failure. But she wrote me to share the news that in Christ she had found freedom. She found moral strength to break old habits, inner healing for the hates and hurts and bitter memories, and courage to make restitutions, clear up entanglements, and hope in God for the future. It read like a case study in spiritual transformation.

Again, I do not believe in magic. And I am not so naïve as to assume that the troubles, struggles, and failures of this woman faded into the past as she finished her letter of testimony. However, I believe the transforming power of Christ was evident in her life. The Son of God, "in the likeness of sinful flesh and for sin," had entered the arena of her futile fight against the law of sin and death; he had gained a victory she could never achieve on her own. I will never forget how I felt as I read this woman's contemporary witness to the "law of the Spirit of life in Christ Jesus" that sets us "free from the law of sin and death" (Rom. 8:2). To that freedom my own spirit and my own experience bear confirming witness.

• A Final Note on Paul and Law

Let me share one more note on the struggles of Paul reflected in Romans 7. Some interpret verses 13–24 as describing Paul's struggle with the carnal mind after his conversion. They believe this passage illustrates the inward spiritual warfare that continues in the life of every believer.

Others also see the passage reflecting the struggle of a Christian with the carnal mind; but they believe this struggle is brought to victorious end in the experience of sanctification, portrayed in Romans 8.

Others see verses 13–24 as depicting mankind in general, mankind in Adam. They believe the passage describes the dilemma of a person awakened under the law, apart from the grace of God. (In this case, *law* means not only the Mosaic law, but also the witness it bears to God's will and presence in whatever laws or principles are behind the development of conscience or morality in society.)

Still others see in the passage a testimony to Paul's personal preconversion struggle with the law. They conclude that law had awakened his conscience, not only to his failures, but to the power of sin against which he had no effective resistance. In this view, the lament, "Wretched man that I am," does not reflect the current experience of the apostle as he is writing. It is not the cry of the Christian Paul. Rather, it is a cry wrung from the heart of every person whom sin and law have brought to despair.

I have to agree with this last view. In the struggle described in Romans 7, there is no hint of Christ's gift of grace, of forgiveness, of the help of the Holy Spirit. The man described is an awakened sinner, striving vainly to do the good—in himself.

However, there is some truth in each of the interpretations. In us humans there is a dynamic tension between sin and grace, law and works. This is so because we live "between the times," between the "already" of our redemption and the "not yet" of our glorification. I am reminded of the sinner who is trying to do right in the face of all the pressures, within and without, to the contrary.

There is victory for that person in Jesus. I think of the believer, struggling with the carnal mind, fighting the battles carnal Christians fight with the powerful patterns of the old-self life that "does not submit to God's law" (Rom. 8:7). There is victory for that believer in the liberating, sanctifying Spirit of Christ. And I think of the Spirit-filled Christian who knows the reality of human weakness, who knows there are no magic ways to a life that is holy, who knows both the power of the Spirit and the reality of living in the body with its needs and its desires. There is victory in the continuing journey of that Christian in constant reliance upon the cleansing, empowering presence of the Spirit of Christ.

In these ways, the words of Paul in Romans 7 still speak to me. I cannot pass over them lightly as if they had no continuing relevance to me. I read Romans 7, bow my head, open my heart, and say, "Yes, I know." Then I read in Romans 8 of the victory that is mine in the Holy Spirit. I open my heart, lift my head, and say, "Yes, I know!"

• Discussion Questions

1. In your own words define or describe the "law of sin and death."
2. Recall if you can a personal experience that awakened you to the power of sin.
3. How do you react to the idea that sin is a power? For some, this means that all of life is seen in terms of spiritual warfare between God and Satan or between the Spirit of God and "secular humanism." How do you respond to this?
4. From Paul's point of view, what is the problem with the law?
5. I have used John's idea of "world" (1 John 2:16) to illustrate Paul's idea of sin. What do you think Scripture means by "the world"?
6. How would you define *flesh* as Paul uses it in Romans 7–8?
7. I have said several times, "We don't believe in magic." What is the difference between magic and the victory Christ wins?
8. How do you respond to the way I have written about the "anticlimax" at the close of Romans 7? Why is it important?

CHAPTER · 9

Life in the Spirit

God has done what the law, weakened by the flesh, could not do: sending his own Son in the likeness of sinful flesh and for sin, he condemned sin in the flesh, in order that the just requirement of the law might be fulfilled in us, who walk not according to the flesh but according to the Spirit. . . .

But you are not in the flesh, you are in the Spirit, if in fact the Spirit of God dwells in you. Any one who does not have the Spirit of Christ does not belong to him. But if Christ is in you, although your bodies are dead because of sin, your spirits are alive because of righteousness. If the Spirit of him who raised Jesus from the dead dwells in you, he who raised Christ Jesus from the dead will give life to your mortal bodies also through his Spirit which dwells in you. . . .

For I am sure that neither death, nor life, nor angels, nor principalities, nor things present, nor things to come, nor powers, nor height, nor depth, nor anything else in all creation, will be able to separate us from the love of God in Christ Jesus our Lord (Rom. 8:3–4, 9–11, 38–39).

● I had been preaching from Romans for a Spiritual Emphasis Week at a Christian college. In a discussion group one day I was asked one clear, direct question I will never forget: "Just exactly what does *sanctification* mean to you?"

I do not remember "just exactly" how I answered at the time; but I have thought a lot about it since then. The first thing I wish to do is eliminate the word *exactly*. I do not know how to deal with any of the great realities of our faith *exactly*. If you will permit me to delete that word, I would like to respond to the question on the basis of Romans 6–8.

The good news of the gospel is that we who have been created in the image of God, but who have sinned and fallen short of the glory of God, have been brought back into right relationship with him by grace through faith. God in Jesus has come to us in the redeeming love of the cross and treats us, not as his enemies, but as his friends. "Since we are justified by faith, we have peace with God" (Rom. 5:1). God meets us sinners in Christ in justifying grace. But that is not where he leaves us. God can do more with sin than forgive it. I believe that with the transition question of Romans 6:1 ("What shall we say then?") Paul begins to draw out the meaning and the implications of being the justified and reconciled children of God.

In chapter 6, our life in Christ is related to sin. In chapter 7, it is related to law. And in chapter 8, the Christian life is related to the Spirit. I believe that in these chapters, Paul's thought progression leads from justification to sanctification. With this Scripture background in mind, what does sanctification mean to me?

• An End to Sin's Tyranny

For one thing, it means the breakup of the tyranny of the old-self life as I identify with Christ in his death and my resurrection with him. I must die to the old sovereign of self, the carnal mind. He who through death brings me into right relationship with himself brings me to his cross, where my sick and disordered self submits to his radical surgery and re-creation.

Sanctification means a life of yieldness to God. In the way that the old flow of death controlled life, so now—in continuing presentation of my whole life to God—the new life of the resurrection produces "righteousness for sanctification" (6:19).

Sanctification means freedom from the bondage of law. My death with Christ means freedom from stifling bondage to external conformity as a means of producing righteousness. I am released from legalism. My sharing of the life of Christ means freedom "from the law of sin and death" (8:2). The awful depths of sin have been plumbed, sin's awesome power has been broken, and now I am free from sin's dominion. They are truths I deeply believe and, by grace, truly experience in my life.

• Power and Weakness

We now come to Romans 8 to learn again that, as we live out our lives in the Spirit in the context of earthly existence, God is for us. Two great realities characterize this wonderful chapter. One is the reality of our power, our victory, and our glory. The other is the reality of our weakness, our humanness, and our limitation. These are not sequential; they are simultaneous.

We know about the triumph that is expressed in this chapter. But do we know that words like "mortal bodies," "suffering," "groaning," "weakness," "tribulation," "distress," "famine, nakedness, peril, and sword" are a part of this same chapter? Both aspects of Christian life—power and peril—continue to exist in us. The Christian life is lived in tension because it is life between the times. It is life in the world and not of the world at the same time. The victory that is ours through the sanctifying power of the Holy Spirit is real; but it is not absolute. We believe that the living God through Jesus makes real changes in our lives; but we do not believe in magic. We are not deceived about ourselves as we live in the Spirit in a fallen world. All human victories, though real, are partial. Our life shares both the reality of human existence and the power of the Lord of glory—and that glory is often incognito. We are not delivered out of our troubles and our struggles, but we share the glory of God in the midst of them. We live at the Cross in the power of the Resurrection. Each human victory, won in the Spirit, is both a reality in itself and a sign/promise of the final victory at the end of the age. No human victory is final or absolute, because we are still on the journey.

Living "between the times" is a helpful concept for me as I seek to understand and live life in the Spirit. We are living, for example, between the times of the first coming and the second coming of Jesus. In him the age to come has overlapped this present age. Jesus has brought into our world the power of the life to come. Yet this present age is still present. His kingdom has come, but that kingdom is not consummated. His grace has come, but the glory of that grace is yet to be. So here we are, living in between. We don't really know whether we are chronologically closer to the first coming or to the second coming. But we know that Christ has not come back yet—and we are here on our journey to meet him.

When I was young, our church occasionally had a prophecy preacher come to tell us that the Lord was coming soon. There were charts and illustrations and all that. The old saints would be blessed, saying, "Amen, Lord, come!" I would be thinking, *Just my luck! About the time I fall in love and get married and all that good stuff, the Lord will come! Story of my life.* Well, now I find myself on the side of the "Amen, Lord, come!" folks. (I'll let the young ones worry about the "good stuff" they will miss.)

The life we live is between the times. It is between our own birth and our own death. Some of us are nearer to our death than to our birth—who knows? We are in between, on the journey, in the process of growing. We are in between what we are and what, by God's grace, we will become; between what grace has done for us and what glory will do. We live in the tension and the stress of our humanness; we share the power of the world to come, while great gifts of the Spirit are coming to us from God.

• The Gift of Assurance

One of them is found in Romans 8:14–16. "For all who are led by the Spirit of God are sons of God. For you did not receive the spirit of slavery to fall back into fear, but you have received the spirit of sonship. When we cry, 'Abba! Father!' it is the Spirit himself bearing witness with our spirit that we are children of God." Earthen vessels that we are, limited in our knowledge and understanding, we yet have the witness of the Spirit assuring us that we are the children of God. We are welcomed into a relationship with the Father like that of Jesus with his Father. Jesus lived as though God were his Father. He acted like it—because it was true. His word for his Father was *Abba,* the Aramaic language's most familiar word for father, connoting family, warmth, and confidence. Paul says that we have received the spirit of sonship so that we, too, cry, "Abba, Father." In this confident cry, the Spirit is bearing witness with our spirits that we are the children of God (8:16). "And because you are sons, God has sent the Spirit of his Son into our hearts, crying, 'Abba! Father!'" (Gal. 4:6).

Some of us have come to Christ as adults through a radical experience of being "born again." When we are asked when we were converted or how we know we are Christians, the answer is usually related to our experience of being "born again." Others of us have grown up in the fellowship of the church and remember that we have always lived in the body of believers. In such cases, our "conversion" or "born again" experiences are not so radical. E. Stanley Jones spoke of conversion as the opening of a flower to the sun. I think of it as the opening of a silent door to fellowship with the One who knocks. It is the heart's "Of course!" or "Yes" to the gentle pressure of the Spirit toward Christ. So where does assurance rest? In experience? Well, yes and no. It is here that the words of Paul come alive to me.

I remember walking around the square of a park nearby a church I was pastoring. It was early morning, and I was trying to memorize Romans 8 in the beautiful language of the King James Version, working on verses 12–17. Over and over, I repeated: "Ye have received the Spirit of adoption, whereby we cry, Abba, Father. The Spirit itself beareth witness with our spirit, that we are the children of God." Somewhere during this repetition the reality of this assurance came home to me in a new way. I realized that my *heart* was saying, "Abba, Father." The "Abba, Father" relationship was mine.

I understood that my saying "Father" was not my own doing; it was the gift of the Spirit to me. I knew myself to be the child of

God because the Spirit was bearing witness to the "Father" relationship with God that was mine in Jesus.

That was certainly not the time I was "born again"; but it was a time of deep insight for me and renewal of confident assurance. My heart is saying "Father" now as I write. Those verses and the insight they brought to me were memorized more than thirty years ago. But they are more true for me now than then. I have realized that the "assurance of salvation" or the "assurance of being born again" is not a special, temporary gift of God to the newly converted. It is the continuing gift of the Spirit to all of us who walk in fellowship with him.

What a wonderful thing it is to live in the assurance that you are a child of God! It means that you know who you are. The sense of sonship is incredibly significant for your life. How you view yourself as a person affects deeply your responses to the world around you and the persons around you.

Every industrial and technological advance since the Enlightenment has diminished our sense of personal worth. Persons are treated as machines to be used for production and are casually replaced when redundant, obsolete, or worn out. But we Christians know who we are. Our worth is not predicated on our market value or production rate. We are children of God who have an intimate, confident, trusting relationship with our Father—like Jesus had. That ever-increasing confidence brings strength and stability for us who live between the times.

• The Gift of Intercession

Another of the great gifts coming our way from God is that his "Spirit helps us in our weakness; for we do not know how to pray as we ought, but the Spirit himself intercedes for us with sighs too deep for words. And he who searches the hearts of men knows what is the mind of the Spirit, because the Spirit intercedes for the saints according to the will of God" (8:26–27). Though we share the creature's bondage to corruption, the Spirit helps us in our weakness and interprets our praying to God. Paul's word about "sighs too deep for words" and the Spirit's making intercession for us is mentioned in the context of three "groanings" (KJV).

He says the whole creation "waits with eager longing for the revealing of the sons of God"; and it "has been groaning in travail together until now" (8:19, 22). I wonder, if we had ears to hear and hearts to feel, would we hear the groaning of creation as it bears the burden of the curse of mankind's sin? Do the hills groan under the defacing blades that carve out space for the houses of the profiteering land developers? Does the earth ever groan as its bowels are torn by the nuclear blasts of underground testing? Do the hop and grain fields and the vineyards cry inwardly for the hurt and sorrow and death their fruit will bear? Who cries for the bombed cities, for blasted hopes and dreams? Who weeps for the Eden our planet could have been? The whole creation does. And the loving Creator does!

Under the groaning are creation's hope of restoration, its aspiration for freedom "from its bondage to decay," and its anticipation of "the glorious liberty of the children of God" (8:21). The creation groans and waits in hope. The Creator groans and works in patient, redeeming love.

And the children of God groan as they wait for the redemption of their bodies. We don't have to be very old or experienced to know something of the painful, fragile character of our human existence. Being a Christian is a good life; but its goodness is laced with sorrow and sickness and decay. The times we are together with friends and family for reunions and holidays are precious times. What will another year bring? Mostly we gather for weddings—and for funerals. And every year we learn that someone has moved, someone has died, someone is hurt, someone is sick. We long for a quality of life and fellowship that is not torn by loss. In our transiency, we long for permanence; in our sickness, we long for health. Caught in the inevitable cycle of birth, growth, decay, and death, we yearn for the redemption of our bodies. Thus, we live between the times. We experience the renewing of the inner man even as the outer man is perishing; and we long for the time when the whole man will be restored in the image of God. It is our hope—our living, certain hope—that such a restoration will come. While we wait, we share the groanings of the rest of the created order.

The searching, interceding Holy Spirit also groans. The Holy Spirit who searches our hearts, who knows the mind of God and knows the depths of our human condition, is the one who interprets our praying in the Father's presence. It helps me to know it is Paul who says that "we do not know how to pray as we ought" (8:26). If the apostle Paul, the original "prayer warrior," says that, I feel encouraged. I have been a Christian for more than half a century, but I must confess that I do not know how to pray as I ought. My problem is not that I don't know to pray. (I was a college chaplain for fourteen years, and chaplains either invoke or benedict on all auspicious occasions!) My problem is that I don't know how to pray about the things that matter most to me. When my children were little, I prayed little prayers for little people: "Lord, bless the children. Keep them well. Give them a happy day and help them to grow up to love you." But my children are grown. Now what do I pray for them? The little prayers won't do; but when I try to pray the big prayers, I don't know what to say.

How do you pray for your grown children? For that matter, how do you pray for your pastor or church or missionaries or leaders of world governments? How do you pray when you learn of great world sorrow and hunger and hostility and death?

The Holy Spirit knows me through and through. So he takes the unutterable yearnings of the depths of my heart and, knowing the Father's heart, interprets them according to his will. I do not have to "say it right" in order to pray aright. I may pour out my heart before the Father in the confidence that my Intercessor is also my Interpreter. This means that my thoughts and feelings are not closed off from prayer, even though they may not be "proper."

Sometimes I wonder, *Is it all right to pray about this? I really would be embarrassed to pray about something as petty as this. How can I pray about something I am not even sure is right?* But the Spirit would lead me to honesty in prayer. Some things may indeed be unworthy of prayer; some prayers may be childish or immature or selfish. But if I only pray what I deem to be proper, then I become the judge of what is truly prayable and acceptable to God.

The Spirit is our interpreter. We may pour out our hearts—the good and the bad, the mature and the immature, the selfless and the selfish, the clean and the unclean—we may open up the whole of our hearts to him, for he searches and knows our hearts and interprets our prayers before the Father. The Holy Spirit, with "sighs too deep for words," carries our prayers from the depths of our hearts to the depths of the Father's heart, where he interprets them according to the Father's will.

While the Spirit of God is working within us to interpret our praying, Romans 8:28 tells us that the providence of God is working "outside" us, in all the affairs of our lives, to accomplish good: "We know that in everything God works for good with those who love him, who are called according to his purpose." Caught as we are in the limitations and the determinisms of our human lives, we may know that God is at work for good.

There are some common interpretations of this verse that I do not believe. I do not believe that it means everything is going to turn out right for the Christian in the end. It does not mean that "every cloud has a silver lining" or that "things will balance out" if we have the right attitude. Nor does it mean that what looks like evil is really good in disguise. I cannot agree with those who would praise God for all things equally, without regard for the fundamental distinction between good and evil.

Here is what I do believe. Though many things that happen are not in accordance with God's will, nothing happens that is outside it—that is, outside the area where God is at work in judgment and in creative, healing power. I gathered this concept from a book on Romans by John Knox. I believe it is true: Nothing ever happens outside the judging, redeeming, healing, creative work of God. Nothing is ever too late, too much, too far, too long, for the love of God to work. As Edwin Lewis has said, the Creator has more to give than the Adversary—and he gives it. The creative and healing God is actively at work for good in every situation.

Take, for example, divorce. We know that divorce is wrong and destructive and not God's will. The same could be said of cancer, violent death, or other loss. Yet out of such experiences—through them, in spite of them—new and beautiful things can come. This does not mean that divorce is a good thing in disguise; it means that God is still creating new and beautiful things amid the divorce. Both realities are continuing realities.

Evil and destructive things are not good things covered with dark masks, which God removes to reveal the hidden beauty. Evil circumstance is not merely a cocoon opened so that the butterfly may emerge. Rather, the creative God is at work in evil—in judgment, to be sure, but also in creative, healing power. He does a new work of goodness despite the destructive effects of evil.

The great chapter of Romans 8 climaxes in a hymn of praise for the love of God that never fails. In all the human situation, Paul declares, God is for us. We cannot be separated from his love. He is for us in his deep and intimate knowledge of us. His personal knowing is always ahead of us, always before us, always previous to us. The God who knows us has destined us to be like Jesus, to be conformed to the image of his Son. All along the way, from God's knowing us to his glorifying us, he is faithful.

There is no break in the golden chain of grace. We are not left to ourselves anywhere along the way.

There are no gaps in the saving purposes of God. Never does he say to us, "I have brought you to this place. Now carry on and I will meet you at the Gates."

We are predestined to be like Jesus. And the knowing God who thus predestines us is the one who calls, who justifies, and whose present glory in our lives is our guarantee of our sharing the final glory with him. He is with us all the way. Not anyone or anything can ever separate us from his love. The Father spared not his Son to save us. That is the greatest gift that comprehends all the lesser gifts. God has justified us; so who can bring any charge against us? Christ has died for us; so who can condemn us? Christ has been raised from the dead and intercedes for us; so there is freedom from the accusing, condemning voices.

In verses 35–36, Paul reviews some things that can happen to us. In verses 38–39, he speaks of forces that could be set against us. Then he gives the assurance that we are in God's love forever.

The last portion of this beautiful chapter of life in the Spirit tells me that the winds of God are still blowing. I open my small sails to those winds of grace. The currents of God are still flowing. I surrender my life to the stream of the Spirit. He will not ever let me go; he will not ever let you go. "What then shall we say to this? If God is for us, who is against us? He who did not spare his own Son but gave him up for us all, will he not also give us all things with him?" (8:31–32).

● Discussion Questions

1. I was asked, "Just exactly what does *sanctification* mean to you?" What do you think Paul means when he uses the term? How would you begin to answer the question?
2. How do you respond to the idea of living "between the times"? In what ways does it clarify the nature of our present Christian life?
3. From Romans 8 and from your own experience or understanding, what is meant by the Bible's declaration that the Spirit "bears witness with our spirit that we are children of God"?
4. What does Paul mean when he says that the creation "groans"?
5. When it comes right down to it, how does the Spirit help us in our weakness and in our not knowing how to pray?
6. I don't believe that Romans 8:28 means that everything is going to turn out to our satisfaction. What do you think?
7. Why is it hard for us to believe that God is really for us and that nothing can separate us from his love?

CHAPTER · 10

God's Faithfulness and God's People

They are Israelites, and to them belong the sonship, the glory, the covenants, the giving of the law, the worship, and the promises; to them belong the patriarchs, and of their race, according to the flesh, is the Christ. God who is over all be blessed for ever. Amen. . . .

But of Israel he says, "All day long I have held out my hands to a disobedient and contrary people."

I ask, then, has God rejected his people? By no means! . . . God has not rejected his people whom he foreknew. . . .

But through their trespass salvation has come to the Gentiles. . . . if you have been cut from what is by nature a wild olive tree, and grafted, contrary to nature, into a cultivated olive tree, how much more will these natural branches be grafted back into their own olive tree. . . .

Just as you were once disobedient to God but now have received mercy because of their disobedience, so they have now been disobedient in order that by the mercy shown to you they also may receive mercy. For God has consigned all men to disobedience, that he may have mercy upon all.

O the depth of the riches and wisdom and knowledge of God! (Rom. 9:4–5; 10:21; 11:1–2, 11, 24, 30–33).

● Chapters 9–11 of Romans are hard to understand. They begin with a marvelous song of praise, in which we are assured that nothing "in all creation, will be able to separate us from the love of God in Christ Jesus our Lord" (8:39). They also close with an ecstatic burst of praise: "O the depth of the riches and wisdom and

102

knowledge of God! . . . For from him and through him and to him are all things. To him be glory for ever. Amen" (11:33, 36). So nothing Paul says between these two hymns of praise should be interpreted as denying or diminishing the reality of the saving grace of the sovereign God for all mankind.

Nowhere has the apostle forgotten the theme of his letter, "For I am not ashamed of the gospel: it is the power of God for salvation to every one who has faith, to the Jew first and also to the Greek. For in it the righteousness of God is revealed through faith for faith" (Rom. 1:16—17). William Greathouse has reminded us that all the way through Romans the righteousness of God is revealed. It is true in these chapters as well; they are in continuity with the development of Paul's thought in chapters 1—8 and on to the close of the letter.

Clearly, however, he is dealing in these chapters with a special problem related to his own people, the Jews. The problem could be briefly stated like this: God has chosen Israel to be the people through whom salvation should come to the world. From Israel has come the Savior, the Christ. However, Israel has rejected the very Christ through whom salvation is offered to the world. Israel, the elect people of God, has rejected the elect Son of God. So what is to become of them?

There is much more involved than the question of the destiny of the Jews who have rejected Jesus. It is not really a matter of whether or not the Jews will be saved or, as some have wrongly thought, a question of who is predestined to be saved and who is predestined to be lost. The question is, finally, *Does God keep his Word?* Can we really trust God to make promises and keep them in the face of the rejection of the very people he chose to fulfill them? Can we trust the ability of God to work out his purposes of salvation in a world that has fallen into rebellion against him? If Israel, with all its benefits, can be lost, what hope is there for us with all our weaknesses and failures? What about Israel? is a real question. What about us all? is a more painful question. Paul deals with both questions in these chapters.

• The Background to the Problem

Some review of "Bible basics" may help to put Israel's situation in perspective and give us a starting point for understanding the issues dealt with in Romans 9–11:

1. We are the creatures of God's creation, made in his image but fallen away from him, turned in upon ourselves, and under the power of sin from which we cannot break free.

2. God undertook to do what we cannot do for ourselves. He has come to save us. To do this, he has entered into history. He has involved himself savingly with his disobedient children.

3. In this process, he has called a people we have come to know as Israel. He did not call them because they were anything special. He did not look over mankind and find the finest specimens and say to them, "I have finally found the kind of people I can use." Rather, he chose Abraham, a most human and fallible fellow, and said to him, "I will make of you a great nation and through you all nations will be blessed" (see Gen. 12:2). The uniqueness of the people thus created did not consist of the fact that they were bigger or better or more religious or virtuous or trustworthy than any other nations of the earth. They were special because God, in sovereign grace, created and called them to be his people. Their uniqueness consisted of the fact that they were the people *to* whom God spoke and the people *through* whom he would speak the saving word to the whole world.

4. God's intention in "saving" Israel was not that Israel be saved, but that the world be saved, including Israel. Their chosenness did not exempt them from God's judgment. In fact, their own prophets reminded them that their judgment would be more harsh because they had disdained the privileges of the unique calling that was theirs (Amos 3:2).

5. As it turned out, Israel never became the "light to the nations" (Isa. 49:6), the missionary people God called them to be. They interpreted their election in terms of privilege instead of servanthood. They saw themselves as God's own chosen instead of God's own instruments.

6. In spite of that, and through the "many dangers, toils, and snares" of their history, the covenant-keeping God worked to fulfill his saving purposes through Israel in the coming of Jesus, the Messiah. In this sense, the purposes of God's choice of Israel have been fulfilled—out of the nation, the Savior has come who indeed brings salvation to the ends of the earth.

If we look at it this way, our opening question seems easy to answer. Israel was called for a mission. In spite of themselves, their mission was fulfilled through themselves in Jesus. Since they then rejected Jesus, the nation of Israel can be discarded as a vehicle of world redemption. It can be rendered obsolete and treated the same as any other sinful nation. God now goes on with his saving purposes through the new Israel of faith, the church. Having forfeited any special consideration, Israel is simply one of the nations of the world to which the gospel is to be preached.

The apostle Paul could not hold such a view for at least two reasons. First, he was a Jew who loved his fellow countrymen and could not bear to see them cast aside. Like Moses, he cried, "Alas, this people have sinned a great sin. . . . But now, if thou wilt forgive their sin—and if not, blot me, I pray thee, out of thy book which thou hast written" (Exod. 32:31–32). We don't often see this side of Paul. His identification with his own people was such that, if he could, he would be willing to be lost for them to be saved. But, second, Paul believed it was not only his own people Israel who were at stake; God's purposes and character were also. God had made a promise and covenant with Abraham. At Mount Sinai, God entered into covenant relationship with his people, the family of Abraham. There they became the covenant people of God, who said, "I will be your God. You will be my people." And his Word cannot be broken.

• Faithful to the Covenant

A *covenant* is different from a contract. A contract is between parties who are more or less equal. Each party to the contract makes promises and obligations that are drawn up, signed, and notarized. Each party expects the other to keep his or her part of the contract. If either party breaks the agreement, the contract is void, and the other party is no longer held by the stipulations. But a covenant is not a matter of "the party of the first part and the party of the second part." You have instead "the party of the Creator part and the party of the created part"; "the party of the Redeemer part and the party of the redeemed part"; "the party of the Helper, Deliverer, loving Savior part" and "the party of the helpless slaves and nobodies part."

The Bible reminds us that neither the people of Israel nor their hero leaders were constant in their faithful loyalty to the covenant promises they made to God. But God was always faithful to the covenant promises he made. So the covenant remained in force because of the character of God. He was the faithful God. He had made a promise to Abraham, and he would be faithful through the changing historical situations and the fluctuating human commitments of his chosen people.

Centuries later, the prophets warned the people of Israel that their persistently disdainful disobedience to the covenant had stretched and strained it to the breaking point. And it finally did break. That was the message of Amos, Hosea, Isaiah, Micah, Jeremiah, and Ezekiel. Each declared that God's people had finally broken God's covenant beyond repair. And judgment came. The character of the rejected God is such that, when there was no more hope of repentance in the rebellious people, he said, "I love you like Hosea loves Gomer; I mourn for you like Jeremiah mourns for you; I love you like Ezekiel loves his lost wife and homeland. For my name's sake, for my love's sake, for the sake of my holiness, I will make a new covenant. I will restore and renew and bring you back. And I will give you a new heart to go with your new land."

That is not contract—that is covenant. Its validity does not rest on both parties' consistent fulfillment of the contracted stipulations; it rests on the character, the patient love, and the loyal commitment of the covenant partners, particularly of the superior partner in the covenant.

Paul says that God's covenant promises were not made casually; he will be faithful to his Word, regardless of our response. This fundamental truth has significance for Israel as a nation and for us. If God could not see his promise through because of Israel's fickle response, then he cannot see us through, either. If God's choice to bring salvation to the world through Israel could be sabotaged by Israel's rejection, then his choice of the Christ, the Messiah of Israel, could also be sabotaged by our rejection. Such possibilities are totally out of the question for Paul. God is utterly faithful to his promises. This is the fundamental truth underlying the movement of thought through chapters 9–11.

God's faithfulness to his people is sure. But in chapter 9, Paul makes it clear that "his people" are not his by virtue of having been born to a certain family. Key verses in this chapter are these: "Not all who are descended from Israel belong to Israel, and not all are children of Abraham because they are his descendants" (vv. 6–7). Abraham and his descendants were chosen by the free, loving initiative of God. If the continuity of the chosen people depended simply on biological descent, the promise would effectively be taken out of God's hands. He would be left with the task of following along after the fact, working out his will with whoever happened to be born. This would hardly constitute the true "Israel of God."

Paul gives two illustrations that bear this out. Ishmael was born before Isaac, but Ishmael was not "chosen" simply because he was born first. Esau was born before Jacob, but that fact did not make him the promised descendant. The true Israel is not a matter of physical birth; it is a matter of God's continuing gracious promise. Paul's point is that if some who were physical descendants of the patriarchs rejected the promise, that promise is not thereby put in jeopardy.

Furthermore, since God's choice of Israel is not biological, he is not limited to the Jewish race in his salvation plans. Though God's gracious initiative began with the calling of Abraham, it can continue with his calling of other peoples and other nations as well. The God who calls "people who are not a people" and makes them a people (the Jews) can call others (Gentiles) and creatively incorporate them into his called people (the church) (see 1 Peter 2:9–10).

Some of Paul's language does not fall easily on our ears. Evidently, it did not fall easily on the ears of some of his first readers, either. However, his truth needs to fall heavily on our hearts. We who are children of the Enlightenment, who think that we have things increasingly within the grasp of our understanding and therefore under our control, need to bow again before the mystery of God and his providence. We are not creators; we are creatures. God is still God. My Granddad would say, "God is still on the throne, and he ain't a-aimin' to vacate!"

● Chosen But Unworthy

It is hard for us to recognize that our thoughts about who God is and what he ought to do and how he ought to respond to us are more indicative of our fallenness than of our enlightenment. But we must let God be God and know that the heritage we have as his children—a heritage that goes all the way back to beyond father Abraham—is the product of the Father's gracious purpose, not of biology. We have no right to call Abraham our father; we have no right to be included in the family of God. He did not choose the Israelites because they were worthy. By the same token, he has not opened the door of salvation to Gentiles because they are worthy. We are redeemed children and heirs of the promise only by his sovereign grace.

Our responses, as Jew or Gentile, can only be praise and wonder in the presence of such grace. It is grace that will never fail; it is a saving purpose that will never be ultimately thwarted, because the God who calls us is the one who is with us throughout our history.

When God seems to have failed and his purposes appear to be

nullified by the awesomely destructive forces of our society, we can be sure that he is still God.

But what about the Jews? What has gone wrong with God's plans for them? Paul shows that they turned away from God, not because they had not heard, but because they had not believed. In the beautiful and familiar verses of 10:14–17, we see the tremendous significance of both preaching and hearing: "But how are men to call upon him in whom they have not believed? And how are they to believe in him of whom they have never heard? And how are they to hear without a preacher? . . . So faith comes from what is heard, and what is heard comes by the preaching of Christ." In the original language there is no *of* in the phrase, "in him of whom they have never heard." It literally reads, "in him whom they have never heard." Paul's point is that, in genuine Christian preaching, Christ is the one who is speaking in and through the words of the preacher. Paul discusses preaching to explain the response of his fellow Jews to the gospel; but, in doing so, he says some significant things about preaching.

Real Christian preaching must center in Christ. It will draw the hearts and wills of men and women to Christ. It is preaching in which the preacher is susceptible to the very presence of the proclaiming Christ himself. At the same time, we see the importance of hearing. As the proclamation of the gospel is a part of the gospel (2 Cor. 5:18–19), so hearing is fundamental to making a faith response to the gospel.

Israel rejected the Savior, in part because they misunderstood in what sense they were the chosen people. Their chosenness did not consist of biological lineage. They also rejected the Savior because they misunderstood the purpose of the law (Rom. 7; 9:30–10:13). But, in the last part of chapter 10, we see that Israel rejected the Savior because they did not *hear* the gospel; so they were not able to believe it and be saved. On one side of the equation is the *proclamation,* the preaching of Christ in which Christ himself is heard. On the other side is the *listening,* the hearing in which Christ himself is truly heard. In this context, the Spirit is able to inspire the faith that saves.

Once more we ask, What about the Jews? They have rejected Christ. Will they be cut off and forgotten?

Paul can never tolerate such a thought, though the very rejection of the Jews has opened the door to the Gentiles. If the Jewish nation had accepted the messiahship of Jesus, the Gentile mission would not have taken place the way it did. Paul Achtemeier, in his splendid commentary on Romans, appropriately notes, "The olive tree says it all." The olive grower will take wild shoots and graft them into a cultivated tree, and good fruit will be produced. In Paul's analogy, however, natural processes do not prevail. In this symbolic, spiritual tree, *all the branches are grafted!* Israel is not a "natural" branch; it is chosen to be grafted and has, in that sense, become "natural." Yet Israel has rejected the Savior and so has been "cut off." This cutting off of the Jewish nation has made possible the grafting in of the Gentiles to the olive tree. But there is no place for pride or complacency among the Gentiles. Paul's conviction is that Gentiles can, by their disobedience, be cut off as well; he also believes that the Jews, by their faith, can be grafted in again. He hopes that the faithful obedience of the grafted-in Gentiles will inspire the faith of the ungrafted Jews, so that they, too, may become part of the olive tree of salvation. He believes that his own people will do just that. His vision is that the great mercy of God will work with his chosen, rejecting people in such ways that they will finally respond to his love, manifested in Jesus the Savior.

● Paul's Essential Message

We certainly would not say things the way Paul did; sometimes his logic and language are hard to follow. But his basic conclusions are clear. The first is the most difficult for us to grasp: *God is the sovereign Lord who works his saving purposes in history, mostly without our advice!* Remember these lines?

How odd
Of God
To choose
The Jews.

Well, yes, it does seem odd to us. But he did not ask us. We could as well ask, "Why all the *fuss* for the choosing of *us?*" Paul would have us remember who is God and who is creature; who is Lord and who is servant; who is Savior and who is saved; who is the Finder and who are the lost. These are the ponderings that lead to Paul's closing hymn of praise: "O the depth of the riches and wisdom and knowledge of God! How unsearchable are his judgments and how inscrutable his ways!" (11:33).

The second conclusion is that *Israel still has a place in the saving purposes of God in the world.* Paul is speaking not of the salvation or the damnation of any individuals, but of the destiny of the nation Israel. To take his language in these chapters and apply them to the predestining of anyone, either to heaven or to hell, is to totally miss the point of his argument. Further, we must note that he is not balancing out God's wrath with God's grace. I like Achtemeier's apt phrase, when he says there is an "asymmetry of grace" here: Everywhere and always, grace finally is triumphant.

The third conclusion only extends this same truth: *For all the talk of choosing and rejecting, the purposes of God are purposes of mercy and grace.* Back in Romans 3, Paul declared, "For there is no distinction; since all have sinned and fall short of the glory of God, they are justified by his grace as a gift, through the redemption which is in Christ Jesus" (vv. 22–24). That is a parallel to the final words preceding the hymn of praise in chapter 11, "For God has consigned all men to disobedience, that he may have mercy upon all" (v. 32). Finally, we are all alike in our humanity, all alike in our sinfulness, and all alike in our salvation by grace through faith. "Here there is no Greek and Jew, circumcised and uncircumcised, barbarian, Scythian, slave or free, but Christ is all, and is in all" (Col. 3:11, NIV).

• Discussion Questions

1. Many see these chapters as an interruption to the flow of Paul's thought through Romans. What do you think?
2. State in your own words the problem Paul deals with in chapters 9–11. I believe that beneath the Jew-Gentile question is a more basic one: Can God work out his plans for his children even if they reject him? Do you see other questions here?
3. "Israel is God's chosen people." Explain.
4. Summarize the two reasons why Paul believed that Israel could not be finally lost.
5. How is a covenant different from a contract? How does that relate to what Paul is dealing with in these chapters?
6. Discuss how Paul's references to Abraham, Isaac and Ishmael, Jacob and Esau illustrate the fact that the true Israel is created by divine choice, not by biological descent.
7. Discuss Paul's teaching that hearing is as significant as preaching.
8. I believe Paul teaches that Israel misunderstood what it meant to be the people of God. Can we so misunderstand what it means to be his people that God would reject the church as he rejected Israel? Discuss.
9. Explain Paul Achtemeier's statement "the olive tree says it all."

CHAPTER · 11
The Word of Faith

Brethren, my heart's desire and prayer to God for them is that they may be saved. I bear them witness that they have a zeal for God, but it is not enlightened. For, being ignorant of the righteousness that comes from God, and seeking to establish their own, they did not submit to God's righteousness. For Christ is the end of the law, that every one who has faith may be justified.

Moses writes that the man who practices the righteousness which is based on the law shall live by it. But the righteousness based on faith says, Do not say in your heart, "Who will ascend into heaven?" (that is, to bring Christ down) or "Who will descend into the abyss?" (that is, to bring Christ up from the dead). But what does it say? The word is near you, on your lips and in your heart (that is, the word of faith which we preach); because, if you confess with your lips that Jesus is Lord and believe in your heart that God raised him from the dead, you will be saved. For man believes with his heart and so is justified, and he confesses with his lips and so is saved. The scripture says, "No one who believes in him will be put to shame." For there is no distinction between Jew and Greek; the same Lord is Lord of all and bestows his riches upon all who call upon him. For, "every one who calls upon the name of the Lord will be saved" (Rom. 10:1–13).

● Once more the two ways of salvation are opposed: the way of law and the way of faith. Moses said that whoever would find righteousness in the law would have to fulfill the law. If we try to please God on the merit system, a merit system is precisely what we have, and that is all. We would satisfy our consciences by the performance of duty or by telling ourselves that we have done our duty (or done at least as well as others). Our sense of spiritual well-being would be primarily related to our sense of duty, not to our relationship with God in Christ by grace through faith. Therefore, we could feel quite secure in talking about faithfulness in attendance at church, or daily devotions, or tithes and offerings, or cooperation with the church program, or witnessing, or whatever.

A subtle sense of well-being grows when we are good and are faithful. But when that becomes the base for our sense of spiritual satisfaction or fulfillment, we have made a deadly shift from total dependency upon Christ to dependency upon ourselves.

Don't get me wrong. I am not saying that it is not good to be good. The problem is that our goodness easily becomes defensive and smug. I read somewhere that the earnest become dogmatic, the fervent become fanatical and judgmental, the gentle become wavering, the liberal grow lax, and the benevolent become stuffy and condescending.

That's what's the matter with our goodness: It becomes *our* goodness.

In the closing verses of chapter 9, Paul says the Jews sought righteousness by law and not by faith. This placed them in a dilemma. On the one hand, they could not truly produce righteousness by keeping the law; and on the other hand, they lost the true righteousness that only comes by faith because they were pursuing a legalistic goal they could never achieve.

Only when we learn how insufficient is all our goodness—only when we become so dissatisfied with our whole condition that we are willing to cry, "Lord, be merciful to me, a sinner"—will we realize that the gospel speaks to our true condition. Paul says, "Brethren, my heart's desire and prayer to God for them is that they may be saved" (10:1). Remember what we have already said about being "saved"? It means deliverance, freedom, and security; it means being saved from lostness, vanity, meaninglessness, and guilt. It means being protected, cared for, and satisfied. That's what the Jews wanted, but did not obtain. They had "zeal for God," but it was not "enlightened" (10:2), so they were not saved.

Is that descriptive of us in any way? Do we have zeal for God

while still living at the level of duty? Do we strive for righteousness, but have no life, no joy, no blessing and freedom? Are we
going through the motions?

And all the while we are so right in our doctrines. ("Well, thank
God for that," someone will say. "At least we are right." But I am
not sure that is what it is all about, after all. Paul's desire was not
that the Jews be "right," but that they be "saved"!) The real
problem is not false doctrine; it is false dependency. The real
needs are liberation, freedom, security, and wholeness. These
constitute the salvation we cannot achieve.

> Could my tears forever flow,
> Could my zeal no languor know;
> These for sin could not atone;
> Thou must save, and thou alone.
> —*Augustus M. Toplady*

Paul has a saving word for us! "Christ is the end of the law"
(10:4). God has come to us in Jesus and done for us what we can
never do for ourselves. His love "has broken every barrier down."
Now the relationship between God and us is no longer that of
Creditor and debtor, no longer that of Assessor and earner, no
longer that of Judge and defendant. Because the righteousness of
God is revealed in Christ, we are no longer faced with the task of
trying to satisfy the justice of God. We do not have to work at
pleasing him so that he will be benevolent toward us. He has taken
the initiative to come to us, so that we may accept his forgiving
love and mercy. We do not have to win God's favor; we may take
his love and mercy, which are freely offered to us.

I do not believe that we are lying awake nights, thinking of how
to win our salvation by works instead of by the blood of Jesus. But
I do believe that we face the subtle danger of shifting away from
total dependence upon God to dependence on ourselves and our
efforts to please him. The gospel does not advise us to "reach up"
and "keep trying"; it announces to us that Jesus has come all the
way to us in redeeming love.

• A Word of Faith

The saving word Paul gives us is the word of faith. I love the way Paul talks about this. Within the context of the righteousness of faith, we are told what not to say, what to say, and what to believe.

First, we are not to say, "Who will go up to bring him down?" or "Who will go down to bring him up?" He is here. "The word is near you, on your lips and in your heart" (10:8). If we take this seriously, it could make some significant changes in how we think about the gospel and how we pray.

Perhaps I should speak for myself. So much of my praying is saying what Paul tells me not to say: "If only the Lord would come down. O Lord, come! Please come and help us. O God, you know how much we need you. Please come."

We Christians say to one another that we need to "get God on the scene." If only we could get God in our midst, then things would happen that ought to happen; his will would be done; revival would come. A great Old Testament prayer lament in Isaiah 64:1 expresses this common, heartfelt hunger: "O that thou wouldst rend the heavens and come down." We think that if we could only bare our upraised arms in travailing intercession, if we could only lift up holy hands in prayer, we could somehow lay hold of the mighty power of God and bring it to bear upon our desperate condition. Then, we think, we would have the victory.

Don't nod your head in approval, because Paul said, "Don't say that!" The truth is, the heavens have been rent. God himself *has come* all the way to where we are. He has come! He is here. Truth is, God has bared his mighty arm in our behalf, and his arm has won for us the victory (Isa. 52:10; 59:16). The strong Son of God has stepped into the swollen river of our sin and shame, and he has changed the course of the current. And we are still praying, "O God, please, won't you come down and help us?"

I will never forget the days when it become known that our college president had cancer. He was a strong, athletic, highly intelligent and spiritual person, greatly loved by us all. When the students learned how serious it really was, they came to me and insisted, "We can't have this. We need him. We've got to plan prayer chains and get intercession groups going. We've got to get him healed!"

What does a chaplain do at such a time? Part of me was saying yes to their desire for God to come down and heal him. But part of me was being influenced by Romans 10 and the meaning of the gospel. I know what it means for us to pray and to lift up our hearts to call upon God. I also know that, if we think God is up there in heaven somewhere and we need to get him down out of heaven to meet us here where our needs are, we have missed the whole point of the gospel. We have not yet heard the saving word; and for all our holy intentions, we are still functioning on the basis of our own strength, spiritual effort, and pleading to get the divine response we need.

Through those tragic, traumatic days, through the sore testing of our faith and understanding, I learned in a new way what it means to say not, "O God, come down," but, "O God, you are here! You are Lord in life and in death. You are Lord if it goes well, and you are Lord if it does not go well." Our purpose in prayer is not to bring him down. He is already here.

I am thinking in this connection of one of the greatest stories of the prophet Elisha. The king of Syria was fighting against Israel, but the prophet would tell Israel's king of the Syrian plans. The Syrian king learned about it and set out to capture the man of God. The army came by night and surrounded the city of Dothan. In the morning the young attendant of the prophet saw them and cried, "Alas, my master! What shall we do?"

> Then Elisha prayed, and said, "O Lord, I pray thee, open his eyes that he may see." So the Lord opened the eyes of the young man, and he saw; and behold, the mountain was full of horses and chariots of fire round about Elisha (2 Kings 6:17).

The young man's prayer was, "O God, come and do something." The old prophet's prayer was, "O Lord, open his eyes to see that you are here."

The word of Paul is very clear: "Do not say, 'Who will go up to bring him down?'" That kind of prayer is a denial of the Incarnation. In Jesus, God has come into the arena of our human struggles. His incarnation is real. Neither are we to say, "Who will go down to bring him up?" That kind of prayer is really a denial of the Resurrection. God has raised Jesus from the dead. His resurrection is real. He is here. The word of his salvation is near— near as your lips, near as your heart.

How near is God's incarnation? How close his humanity?
How near is God's resurrection? How close his living presence?
Where you are, on your lips, in your heart . . . God is that near.

Second, Paul tells us what we are to say. He expresses it so beautifully: "Confess with your lips that Jesus is Lord" (10:9). That is what we are to say! Jesus, who is incarnate among us, who is risen from the dead, is Lord.

• "Jesus Is Lord"

What do we mean when we say, "Jesus is Lord"? For one thing, it means that we recognize his sovereignty. We affirm that he is in charge, right where we are. He is bigger than what is going on. Our declaration of his lordship is a recognition of his kingship, his sovereignty over the situation.

Perhaps you need to say, in the light of your present condition, "Jesus is Lord." Jesus is sovereign in your situation. Let him be Lord. Accept his lordship at the point of your need, at the point of your failure, discouragement, hopelessness, or despair. He is here and he is sovereign. That fact calls for a shift of attitude or posture that moves the "center of gravity" from yourself to him. If he is sovereign, then you are not. If he is sovereign, then your situation is not. Your circumstance is not omnipotent; it is not all-controlling over you if you recognize who is the real Master.

In the recognition of the mastery of Jesus, I am released from the false servitudes and bondages that would stifle my freedom and joy. I am especially released from the need to bring the divine presence and power into my present condition by my pious efforts and spiritual struggles. He is here and he is Lord.

For another thing, when I say, "Jesus is Lord," it means that I accept his authority. I am saying, "Not my will, but thine, be done" (Luke 22:42). This was the response of Jesus to his Father; it is to be my response to Christ. (What easy words to write!) If I say that Jesus is Lord, I bow down, let go, give over, and say yes to him and to his will. Perhaps I cannot discern his will in some specific situation; but I must adopt this fundamental posture and attitude toward the authority of Jesus.

Here we are not far from the truth of Romans 6: The old self is crucified with him. Self-sovereignty and the sovereign authority of Jesus are not compatible. They cannot—they will not—continue to coexist, maintaining some sort of balance of power. Remember that the context of this entire discussion is the way of faith contrasted with the way of the law. The way of faith is opposed to the way of self-effort. The confession of our lips and our hearts that Jesus is Lord means the end of self-effort and self-sovereignty. *Faith* means trust and obedience. It means trust in Christ's sovereignty; it means obedience to his authority. I learned these words of a chorus in the church where I used to live:

> I'll say, Yes, Lord, Yes,
> To your will and to your way;
> I'll say, Yes, Lord, Yes,
> I will trust you and obey.
> When your Spirit speaks to me,
> With my whole heart I'll agree
> And my answer will be, Yes, Lord, Yes.

A third and marvelous thing it means to say that Jesus is Lord is participation in the power of his resurrection. Anyone who comes under the sovereign authority of Jesus connects with his resurrection power. That is how I understand the closing section of our Scripture passage. It was after the resurrection, the ascension, and the exaltation of Jesus that the Holy Spirit was poured out upon the church. That outpouring of the Spirit certified the lordship of Jesus, who is now exalted at the right hand of the Father. In the experience of the presence of the risen Jesus, in the power of his Spirit, the disciples proclaimed, "Jesus is Lord." If *we* attempt to work out our righteousness by law, morality, conformity, duty, or whatever, we can work only at the level of what we can do. But when Jesus is Lord, his resurrection power is released in us.

● Resurrection Is More Than Life

This talk of resurrection leads us to Paul's word that tells us what to believe: "If you confess with your lips that Jesus is Lord and believe in your heart that God raised him from the dead, you will be saved" (10:9). The saving word is, "Jesus is risen." That is why we are not to say, "Who will go down to bring him back from the dead?" God has reversed the course of nature, brought Jesus back from the dead, and enthroned him in power and glory. That makes *Resurrection* a saving word.

Notice that this is a saving word about sin as much as it is about death. If Easter did nothing more than give us the promise of a deathless life—the way we are—that would not be heaven. The promise of immortality, or endless existence, is of itself no saving word. Think of the disciples after the crucifixion of Jesus. They were utterly devastated, totally discouraged, bitterly disappointed in themselves—and, if we know anything about human nature, defensive and resentful toward one another. They were hiding in an upper room in fear. Who knows where Peter was or what he was thinking? Where was Thomas, and what was he doing? They were isolated and helpless and afraid. What if the news of Jesus' resurrection only let them know that they would live forever? That would only mean an endless lifetime of making excuses, justifying mistakes, bolstering reputations, and proving the rightness of their behavior. Or it would mean an eternity of guilty regret, sorrow, and self-recrimination. For us, such an incomplete promise of resurrection would mean the same thing—the mere continuation of ourselves the way we are.

But the resurrection of Jesus promises us more than endless life.

It promises *victory over sin and self* as well as the grave! We "believe in him that raised from the dead Jesus our Lord, who was put to death for our trespasses and raised for our justification" (Rom. 4:24–25). So the resurrection can make a difference in the inner life. It can cut the nerve of self-centeredness and guilt and anxiety. That transformation begins when the love of God in Jesus, revealed in the cross, is seen to be ultimately triumphant in his resurrection. That is the saving word we need to hear. When Jesus identifies himself with us to the point of dying for our sins, we realize that we are bound up with one another. The fact that God raised Jesus from the dead does not unbind him from us; it unbinds us from the sin and death he came to conquer. Just as he is one with us in our human sin and shame, we are one with him in his resurrection victory.

Can we believe this in our hearts? With our whole selves, can we say yes to this? Do we realize that the lordship of Jesus is exercised in the power of the resurrection? The Christian's experience of and hope for salvation does not rest on a naïve perception of the real world. It does not rest on a shallow attitude toward evil. It rests solidly on the resurrection of Jesus Christ. That is the basis of our hope. Christian hope rests on discernment of the love and power of God that raised Jesus from the dead. The Christian believes that out of death can come life, out of darkness can come light, out of hopelessness and utter despair can come promise and joy by the power of God.

We do not believe that death in some way produces life, that light follows darkness with the inevitability of the dawn, or that joy will ultimately emerge out of despair. Life, light, and joy are the creative gifts of God. Death does not produce life; God does. Darkness does not produce light; God does. We believe this because God raised Jesus from the dead against all the odds.

Nor do we believe that a supernatural life force in the man Jesus stimulated his resurrection. The Father raised his Son from the realities of death and the grave. And so we hope. So we are saved.

I am indebted to James Stewart for this insight into the meaning of Resurrection. Imagine a student of literature working on a sonnet. No inspiration comes. As the deadline approaches, the anguished cry is heard, "O Shakespeare, help me!" Or imagine a statesman struggling with a complex political decision, who calls out in despair, "O Jefferson, help me!" Then imagine the Christian pilgrim on the journey of life, striving vainly against temptation, who prays, "O Jesus, help me!" With that word—"O Jesus"—we are suddenly in another and divine dimension. Shakespeare rests unhearingly under his monument. Jefferson lies deaf in his honored grave. But Jesus is present in power by his Spirit; he yet lives. And his is the strength that defeats the Tempter.

My brother told me of a teenager in his parish who was hopelessly caught in loneliness, drugs, and depression. One day, in total despair, the young man honestly said, "O Jesus, help me." And he did. What wonderful changes began to take place in the young man's life. He experienced real freedom and a new sense of worth by belonging to Christ.

The poet Wordsworth, looking over literary England, cried out in pain, "O Milton, thou shouldst be living at this hour. England hath need of thee. She is a fen of stagnant waters." Stewart notes that sometimes, as we view our dark and desperate world, we find ourselves crying out, "O Jesus, thou shouldst be living at this hour. The world hath need of Thee. She is a fen of stagnant waters." But back comes the answer like a thousand trumpets, "Should be? He is!" For the Lord says, "I am he that liveth, and was dead; and, behold, I am alive for evermore" (Rev. 1:18 KJV).

This saving word is near us. It is in our hearts and on our lips. It is the word of faith, faith that rises out of our hearts and is confessed with our lips, saying, *Jesus is Lord.*

● Discussion Questions

1. We are back again to the problem of law and grace, faith and works. Why does Paul keep bringing up these matters?
2. Discuss the statement "Paul's desire is not that Israel be 'right,' but that Israel be 'saved.'"
3. What is meant by the statement "Christ is the end of the law"?
4. Discuss the comments on what not to pray. In what sense is it right to ask God to "come down"? What are we wanting when we ask that?
5. If we don't have to ask God to come down, what attitude should we have toward prevailing prayer, intercession, or fasting?
6. What do you mean when you say, "Jesus is Lord"?
7. Discuss the idea that Christ's resurrection is as much about sin as it is about death. How does it affect our sin problem?

CHAPTER · 12

Spiritual Worship and the Essential Change

O the depth of the riches and wisdom and knowledge of God! How unsearchable are his judgments and how inscrutable his ways! . . . For from him and through him and to him are all things. To him be glory for ever. Amen. I appeal to you therefore, brethren, by the mercies of God, to present your bodies as a living sacrifice, holy and acceptable to God, which is your spiritual worship. Do not be conformed to this world but be transformed by the renewal of your mind, that you may prove what is the will of God, what is good and acceptable and perfect (11:33–12:2).

● Paul says, "I appeal to you therefore. . . ." I love the proverb: Whenever you find a *therefore* in the Bible, you need to stop and find out what it is there for. Wherefore this *therefore?* It is, in fact, one of a series of significant *therefores* in Romans, which I have come to see as hinges on which the doors of the book swing open.

The first one is in 3:20: "Therefore by the deeds of the law there shall no flesh be justified in his sight" (KJV). This *therefore* speaks of our sinful inability and inadequacy to bring ourselves into right relationship with God by ourselves. Whatever law you want to talk about—the law of Moses, the law of conscience, the law of good works, the law of morality, the law of duty, or whatever—we are sinners and cannot save ourselves by law. This is our fundamental sinful condition. The marvel of the gospel is that God comes into our sinful situation, meets us in costly, redeeming grace, and brings us into right relationship with himself through faith.

"Therefore, since we are justified by faith, we have peace with God through our Lord Jesus Christ" (Rom. 5:1).

Then Paul moves on to talk about dying with Jesus at the cross, yielding our risen selves to God, obtaining freedom from legalism and from the law of sin and death. I see in Romans 8:1 the *therefore* of sanctification or life in the Spirit: "There is therefore now no condemnation to them which are in Christ Jesus, who walk not after the flesh, but after the Spirit" (KJV). See the great mercies of God—justifying mercies, reconciling mercies, regenerating mercies, liberating mercies, sanctifying mercies! Oh, the depth of the riches and wisdom and knowledge of God!

Here is another *therefore:* "I appeal to you therefore, brethren, by the mercies of God, to present your bodies as a living sacrifice, holy and acceptable to God, which is your spiritual worship" (12:1). I have come to understand this *therefore* as one of presentation—not as one that leads to an experience of sanctification or fullness of the Spirit, but one that signifies the giving of our embodied selves that follows from it. This *therefore* opens the door of Paul's discussion of practical Christian life.

● A Penchant for the Practical

The apostle has a way of taking the great truths of the gospel and relating them abruptly to the common life. Ephesians 3, for example, closes with a great doxology. But chapter 4 begins, "I . . . beg you to lead a life worthy of the calling." First Corinthians 15 closes with a marvelous song of triumph over death—"thanks be to God. . . ." But chapter 16 begins, "Now concerning the contribution for the saints. . . ." Paul does the same thing in Romans. The great doxology of 11:33–36 seems to gather up all the great realities of God's gracious revelation of his righteousness in Christ to individuals and to nations, throughout history. Then comes the very next line: "Present your bodies as a living sacrifice." One wonders, *How anticlimactic can you get? Is this what it all comes down to?* It would appear so.

Romans 12:1–2 may not be the most significant verses in the book, but they bear heavily on Paul's purposes for writing the epistle. Whatever he has said about sin, grace, salvation, and the purpose of God in chapters 1–11 must come through the door of 12:1–2 into the Christian life in the real world of church, state, and society. If Romans must be divided into only two parts, these verses are the hinges on which the door closes on one part and opens to the other. Let's think about them from this perspective.

• The Sacrifice of Ourselves

Paul's exhortation is very clear: "Present your bodies as a living sacrifice" (12:1). Christians believe that their bodies belong to God as much as their souls do. Even that is not a good way to express it, because *body* does not refer to the physical body apart from the *soul*. Paul uses the term to mean the embodied self or the ensouled body. He means the whole being—body, soul, spirit— the whole person present in bodily form. So the *body* is not just skin and bones, but, for Paul, includes the skin and bones.

I have thought about it this way: I am not a body, but I have one. If you tried to cut off my hand, I would say, "Don't do that. It's mine." But I would not say, "That's me." However, if you were putting a knife to my neck, I would begin to yell, "That's me!" At that point, I would feel that I and my body were very nearly identified! But I am not a body; I have one. Incidentally, I have to warm it, cool it, wash and dry it, clothe it, feed it, diet it, rest it, exercise it—and take it with me everywhere I go. It can be a burden. But I never am without it.

At the same time I distinguish myself from my body, I realize that I have no perception of myself apart from it; nor do I know any other "self" apart from the body. We speak of the deep, inner spiritual beauty of a person but never know or share that inner, beautiful self without being in the presence of the warm, physical body. The inner spirit is only known through the outer body. Letters won't do it. It doesn't happen over the telephone. Our real selves are known only through our bodies. That is why I like the phrase "our embodied selves."

For this reason, whatever we do for God, we must do in our bodies. At an Ashram I once heard J. T. Seamands say that our bodies are "the swinging doors of our existence." The doors swing inward, and we receive. We see, hear, smell, touch, taste. Through senses we receive perceptions, ideas, and feelings that become the basis of many behaviors and attitudes. On the other hand, the doors swing out, and we give. We send signals through our outer body language, through the look, the smile, the tears. The body is our point of contact with others and our world. So any "spiritual" thing we wish to do must be done with our bodies.

When God, who is spirit, got ready to do the best and "most spiritual" thing he ever did, he came in a body. The announcement of the Savior was made with the promise of a sign: "You will find a babe wrapped in swaddling cloths and lying in a manger" (Luke 2:12). When Jesus came to do the most spiritual thing ever done— to save us from our sins—he "bore our sins in his body on the tree" (1 Peter 2:24). God's point of contact with us is in the incarnate, embodied Lord Jesus. God's point of contact with the world he would save is the church, which is his body.

So Paul says, "Take your body [your embodied self—that is, your real, common ordinary life] and give it to God." All of us have heard that we ought to give God our time, talents, money, and all such. But have we heard the clear call of God to give our bodies to him? That means our physical bodies and all that we do in them. We are not to despise our bodies, reject them, punish them, indulge them, or worship them. We are called to present our embodied selves to God. Have you ever consciously, deliberately done that?

• True Worship

This presentation of our bodies to God is an act of spiritual worship. The word translated *worship* in the RSV is translated *service* in the KJV. It is a word that in the Greek culture of the first century meant "service to the gods." It was never used for the service of men to men. For us, our bodily self-giving is a sacrificial act in the service of God. Our spiritual worship is the offering of our bodies to God. This is a revolutionary idea.

Let's consider worship. When we speak of worship, we usually mean the gathered body of believers on a Sunday morning, with hymns and prayers and Scripture readings and sermon. Perhaps we think of stained-glass windows, organs, choirs, liturgical robes, processionals, and candles. When we speak of spiritual worship, we usually mean prayer and praising, Bible reading and meditation, singing and awareness of the presence of God.

Two things impress me. One is that none of these spiritual worship actions is done without using our bodies. No matter how holy, no matter how spiritual, no matter how heavenly our worship experiences may be, our bodies—these hands, feet, face, and lips—participate. The other thing is that Paul says our true spiritual worship is the giving of our bodies to God.

I heard of a housewife who put a motto over her kitchen sink: DIVINE SERVICE CONDUCTED HERE DAILY. Paul would understand that sentiment. He would encourage us to take our bodies and all the tasks we do every day—the ordinary work of home, school, shop, office, and field—and offer them all as an act of worship. In this way, the declaration that "Jesus is Lord" is understood at the place where life is really lived. Paul challenges us to have a sacramental view of the whole of life. Our ordinary distinctions between sacred and secular are transcended in the presentation of our bodily existence to God.

We should reexamine our common divisions between the sacred and the secular. I am sure such divisions can be valid; but we tend to categorize things in terms of "holy" things or "ministry-related" things. Have you noticed that people involved in "active ministry" (what did we do before that phrase came into vogue?) are usually up-front people who teach, lead, direct, control, supervise, sing, or preach? But what about doing the dishes, mowing the lawn, paying the bills, taking care of the nursery, or setting up the fellowship hall for the potluck dinner? The folks who do these sorts of things are the same ones to fold up the chairs and rearrange the setup for Sunday school classes that the "ministry folks" are going to minister in.

How many students in Christian colleges live in the tension between the homework they need to do and the Bible study or ministry outreach God wants them to do? It is not easy for them to see that their perspective puts God against God; but it does. Understanding chemistry is just as holy as understanding Paul's First Epistle to the Corinthians. (For that matter, it is perhaps a little easier!) A study table is as holy as a communion table, because worship takes place at one as well as the other.

Some Christians say, "I will pray for you." Others say, "What can I do to help?" There was a great old fellow in a church I pastored who, instead of praying, "Lord bless them," would pray, "Give them a hand, Lord. Give them a hand." I often wondered if he could ever say, "Here, Lord, use mine." Truth is, sometimes I need blessing—but a lot of times I need a hand.

I heard about a speaker who looked at his wristwatch and discovered it had stopped. He paused to ask, "Does anyone here have a battery-powered watch?" Hands went up. "Anybody have a little bitty jumper cable?"

That is the kind of ministry we usually need: someone with a hand; someone with a jumper cable; someone with a lift, a phone call, a visit. Do you suppose we can ever learn to offer to God our common life and the ordinary things we do for others as our service to him? The Bible says this is spiritual worship.

I think of the awesome stories Jesus told at the close of his ministry, recorded in Matthew 24–25. Nations are gathered, and the Great Judgment is at hand. On the one hand are those who are welcomed with blessing. God's word to them is, "Come." On the other hand are those who are condemned. The word they hear is, "Go." What divides them? Final destiny is being determined, ultimate issues are at stake; and what is the decisive factor? "I was hungry . . . I was thirsty . . . I was a stranger . . . I was naked . . . I was sick . . . I was in prison . . ." (Matt. 25:35–36). Those who are the lost were busy fulfilling their ministry. And those who had no "ministry" picked up some groceries for the poor folks, gathered up some clothes, dropped by the hospital, and called about the girl in juvenile hall. In the words of the old spiritual, "Sometimes it causes me to tremble, tremble, tremble!"

● The Gospel of Nonconformity

The next stage in the development of Paul's thought is in continuity with what has gone before; it rests on his fundamental call to present our redeemed, embodied selves to God. He says, "Do not be conformed to this world but be transformed by the renewal of your mind, that you may prove what is the will of God, what is good and acceptable and perfect" (12:2). I love the paraphrase of J. B. Phillips: "Don't let the world around you squeeze you into its own mold." (For some reason, when I read these words, I always think of a tube of toothpaste!)

The world exercises a controlling and molding force over every life born into it. The world seeks conformity. The free, independent, nonconforming young person is expected to wear the uniform of the free, independent, non-conforming young person. The clothes, the music, and the entertainment are prescribed for this season's worldlings. What to eat and drink, what to drive, and even what drugs to take are all part of the powerful pattern of conformity. The religion of body worship and its striving, failing devotees reflect this pattern. We see it in bulimia and anorexia. We see it in the rise of teen suicide.

The church also, insofar as it partakes of the character of the institutions of our fallen world, seeks to produce conformity and will exert its power to the limit to impose it. The molding, conforming pressure exercised by the church can be as destructive to the freedom of the Spirit as any such pressure exercised by the social institutions of the world.

Paul makes clear the good news that God does not mold us like the world does. He does not squeeze us into a mold. He remakes us from within. When God wants to make a rose, he does not shape his hand into the form of a rose and stamp them out on the assembly line. He sends the sun, the rain, the soil, the cool nights, and dewy mornings—and the rosebush produces roses from within. That is the way God works with us. He will not form his hand in the shape of a saint, squeeze us into it, and send us out as holy clones. He remakes us from within, by the renewing of our minds. He works with how we think and how we see things.

We have studied enough of the Epistle to the Romans to know that our minds are not free from fallen self-centeredness and willful perversion. Paul denies that God works magic on us or in us. We are what we are because we have let our instinctive desires control us. Our minds are clouded and sometimes confused by subtle, undiscovered patterns of egotism and acquisitive desire. We are no longer able to see clearly what love means. We need some new inner dynamic, some force from within that can continuously and progressively illuminate, cleanse, and renew us.

To use H. H. Farmer's language, "it is our faith and experience that such cleansing and renewing of the inner life are possible!" The Spirit, who searches our hearts and knows the mind of the Father, works from inside us. He does not trample our wills; rather, we feel the inspiration of his cleansing, guiding presence. His goal is to release our true selves in the love and freedom of God. He remakes us from within, increasingly making us more like Jesus, in whom alone our true selves are discovered.

This inner transformation of the mind takes place as we present our bodies to God, which is our spiritual worship. Here is the progression of Paul's thought: (1) In the light of the unsearchable mercies of God, we are to present to him our embodied selves. (2) This bodily presentation is our spiritual worship, which leads to the transformation of our minds. Could it be that transformation of our thinking comes by the giving of our bodies to God? Does a fundamental change of mind-set come from the offering of the common life to him? It would appear so!

Let me put it this way: Do you need some new and good thing in your life? Are you at a time in your journey when you feel that something needs to change? Do you hunger for spiritual renewal or deepening? If we have the idea that these deep hungers will be satisfied by some new "experience," then we must conclude that those who have the great experiences find their fulfillment—and the rest of us do not.

But if I understand the message of the apostle, our need for inner transformation and our desire for a fundamental change of mind-set can be satisfied only by giving our bodies to God. Do you need new spiritual perspective on your job? Give God your job. Do you want to know the good, acceptable, and perfect will of God? Give him your family, your kitchen, your garage; offer to him the place you live and what you do in it; present to him your body and all you do in it.

There have been in my life times of deep hunger for God— yearnings for new awareness of his presence—hungers unsatisfied by my efforts to pray more or read the Bible more. Fulfillment has come when I have lived as unto the Lord. Spiritual change came when I settled down and did a better job teaching, when I sat down and caught up on my correspondence, when I helped Mary Jo with the dishes or finished some nagging repair job around the house. When I mow the lawn, do my homework, and responsibly attend to the duties that are mine to be done in this body— something happens to my soul.

When I get hungry for something new from God, where do I get it? Where do I go? What do I do? What if there is no retreat coming up? What if there is no place to pray, no time to get alone, nowhere to go and "be holy"? This passage of Scripture has a very good word for such a time: *Give God your body.* In colloquial language, "Give your bod to God." That is the spiritual worship that leads to essential change from within. In this way we "prove what is the will of God, . . . good and acceptable and perfect" (12:2).

• Discussion Questions

1. Describe what Paul means by "your bodies" in Romans 12.

2. We are to present our bodies as living sacrifices. Is there any connection here with the sacrifices of animals in the temple?

3. What are some ways we falsely distinguish between the sacred and the secular? Is all distinction between the two to be avoided? Is worship more sacred or holy than caring for the sick in Jesus' name? Can one activity ever take the place of the other? Discuss.

4. We identify spiritual worship and ministry with the up-front, leadership roles. How can we better understand the "ministry" dimension of the ordinary, helpful things we do?

5. In the name of freedom, the world promotes conformity in such matters as dress, behavior, leisure activities, and food. How can we keep the church from doing the same thing?

6. I have understood Romans 12:1–2 to mean that changes in my mindset, transformations in how I think and feel about things, take place as I give God my very physical and bodily life. Discuss.

7. Does giving my bodily life to God have anything to do with finding and doing the will of God? Can a person discover the will of God just by doing unto him the daily things of life? Discuss.

C H A P T E R · 13

The Christian Life

For by the grace given to me I bid every one among you not to think of himself more highly than he ought to think, but to think with sober judgment, each according to the measure of faith which God has assigned him. . . .

Bless those who persecute you; bless and do not curse them. Rejoice with those who rejoice, weep with those who weep. . . .

Let every person be subject to the governing authorities. . . . not only to avoid God's wrath but also for the sake of conscience. . . .

Owe no one anything, except to love one another; for he who loves his neighbor has fulfilled the law. . . .

Put on the Lord Jesus Christ, and make no provision for the flesh, to gratify its desires. . . .

Let not him who eats despise him who abstains, and let not him who abstains pass judgment on him who eats; for God has welcomed him. Who are you to pass judgment on the servant of another? . . .

We who are strong ought to bear with the failings of the weak. . . . that together you may with one voice glorify the God and Father of our Lord Jesus Christ (12:3, 14–15; 13:1, 5, 8, 14; 14:3–4; 15:1, 6).

● The great hymn of praise that glorifies "the riches and wisdom and knowledge of God" (11:33–36) is a climax of Paul's treatment of the mystery of redeeming grace working in the history of sinful men. It is also the introduction to his practical talk about the Christian life. Romans begins with good news instead of good advice. Here Paul has not forgotten his message and shifted to giving good advice. These closing chapters of Romans, filled as they are with exhortations and instructions, flow from the great praise hymn just as surely as the realities of the gospel lead to it.

Behind the "ordinary" ethical advice found in Romans 12–15 are some crucial realities of a radically different sort than the kinds the world perceives. These realities make all the difference between gospel and good advice; they are the "something more." For example, Christians do not act kindly or try to live peaceably so that the world will be a better place in which to live. If we smile at all who pass by or if we hold hands across the country and sing to one another, it is not because we think that thereby a new era of lasting peace will arrive. We do not treat others with respect simply because the human species should take care of itself. Every Christian would value such worthy projects. But the Christian's whole world view is different from other people's; the Christian's ethical and moral behaviors, though often externally very much like those of his contemporaries, are based on profoundly different perceptions of reality.

Behind the exhortations given to Christians in Romans 12 are the great realities of chapters 1–11. Behind Paul's ethical guidance is the profound belief in "God the Father almighty, maker of heaven and earth." Behind them is the understanding that another kingdom is the real kingdom; this other kingdom is the kingdom of God, who has entered into our history in Jesus. His coming discloses the reign of God and brings the false values and ideals of the kingdom of this world under judgment. We Christians believe we are to live in the perceptions, values, and goals of the new era that has dawned in the coming of Christ.

So when Christians endeavor to "be good," it is not to make the world better; it is an expression of the goodness of that better world brought into focus by Jesus' life and teachings, his death and resurrection. Christian ethics express the reality of the reign of God in history. They anticipate the goodness of the rule of God in the final glory.

● Behavior, Character, and Christian Ethics

There is something else. When Christians respond to the ethical advice of Paul in Romans and seek to live it in humility and sincere love, we know that such behavior does not make us any better than anyone else. We also know that our good behavior does not establish any merit with God. There is no accrued goodness—there are no grounds for self-righteousness in the good actions of Christians. We realize we never can, of ourselves, fulfill the exhortations or live up to the advice. So we "think with sober judgment" (12:3), not in self-satisfaction, but in humility.

There is one more thing. When we listen to Paul exhort us to "not be haughty, but associate with the lowly" (Rom. 12:16), we know that we are not merely heeding the advice of one of our great Christian apostles. We are being urged to follow the example of Jesus our Savior, who, "though he was in the form of God, did not count equality with God a thing to be grasped, but emptied himself, taking the form of a servant" (Phil. 2:6–7). The fact that the example is Christ's makes all the difference in our response.

The final question is not, What is Paul telling us to do? It is rather, In the light of what the apostle is saying, what does it mean to be like Jesus?

Obviously, the new life we have in Christ is to be lived out in a new and different way. It is to be lived in the community of believers, which is called the body of Christ. Christ is both the head and the source of life within the body of which we are members. T. W. Manson makes the point that the church is called the body of Christ, not the body of Christians. When Paul speaks of the body of Christ and its members, he is not using a convenient figure of speech. The body is a spiritual reality. We really are one body; we really are members in mutual relations. Leaders in church renewal speak of "body life"; Paul would have us participate in "body ethics." How are we to do this?

1. We need to understand what it means to be part of that body (12:3–13).

2. We relate to those "outside," who may be antagonistic or hostile to Christ and to us (12:14–21).

3. As members of the body of Christ we may not be of the world, but we are in it; so we must find our way within the context of a governmental system (13:1–7).

4. Since we live in the expectation of the coming of Christ, we need to be all the more aware of our debt of love to one another (13:8–14).

5. Love makes possible the resolution of rivalries within the fellowship, so that those who are "strong" do not hurt or take advantage of the "weak" (14:1–23).

Paul's basic concern for the church is voiced in the prayer, "May the God of steadfastness and encouragement grant you to live in such harmony with one another, in accord with Christ Jesus, that together you may with one voice glorify the God and Father of our Lord Jesus Christ" (15:5–6). This small comment, almost hidden in the list of practical exhortations on the Christian life, reflects both the praise of Romans 8:38–39 and the hymn of Romans 11:33–36.

If salvation is by grace, then ethics express our gratitude for that grace. We are to live for the glory of God, after the example and by the power of Christ, in the mood of praise, worship, and joy.

• Being Members of Christ's Body

Romans 12:3 begins with an authoritative call to the individuals of an entire Christian congregation to think humbly and soberly about themselves. "Every one among you" is an important phrase. Paul was writing to a church made up of both Jews and Gentiles. Some members of the church at Rome had a long and revered history of religious life and practice. Others had lately come to the Christian faith and had entered the church out of backgrounds and lifestyles that were scandalous and offensive to the Jewish contingent. But they all had to get along with one another in church. It makes sense, then, that the first practical word to the entire group is a call to humility.

It is easy for us at this distance to misjudge the radical, wrenching adjustment on the part of each group to become one in a single body of believers. But it is always costly for Christians to be one body.

The body of Christ is structured by grace. It works like a body and acts in love. For that to happen, all believers need, in Paul Minear's words, "to cut their ego down to size." I think the apostle Paul would say the same to us.

If we read these verses as merely good advice to Christians, we will leave ourselves unjudged and unhealed. But these are hard verses! Paul is addressing a difficult situation in this early church, specifically in the Roman church. Jews and Gentiles were dissimilar in many ways. This made their fellowship vulnerable to division. There are difficult situations in our modern churches, too. I wonder, are we any more ready to accept outsiders into our fellowship than the Jews were to accept Gentiles?

Minear, in his study of Romans, posed some serious questions in this regard: Have I really given my body as a living sacrifice? Is my self-estimate or self-praise commensurate with God's gift? Do I measure my achievements in terms of grace? How strong is my faith in terms of love?

● Expecting Hostility

Verse 14 introduces "those who persecute you." Was Paul thinking of the words of Jesus in the Sermon on the Mount (Matt. 5:10)? Is Paul speaking here about animosities and antagonisms within the church fellowship, or about the relationship of the church to the outside world? There probably are points on both sides. At least, such solutions as Paul suggests are as effective within the church as outside it. The key verse of the paragraph is verse 18, "If possible, so far as it depends upon you, live peaceably with all."

The new reality to which we are called—the reality of the church—is at odds with the old reality of the world in which we yet live. The values and goals of the two worlds are often at odds with each other, and we are caught in between.

In Paul's day, when the church was young and in definite opposition to both the religious world of Judaism and the political world of Nero's Roman Empire, the Christians knew many "enemies." Who are the enemies within our churches today? Who are the enemies without? These are difficult questions. I think of the old *Pogo* cartoon strip, in which he and his friends are crowded in the little boat. Pogo, wearing his colonial hat, holding aloft the flag tied to his upraised oar, cries out, "We have found the enemy—and he is us!" The enemy is outside the church, but the enemy is also inside the church. And the enemy is inside ourselves. In many cases, the enemy is anyone in whom I see reflected those things I do not like in myself: characteristics I would like to hide or attitudes of which I am secretly ashamed. The enemy is often the one who, in one way or another, is a threat to my sense of place or sense of worth.

Well, how are we to respond to those who are hostile to us? It seems that we are to have the same attitude toward other persons, whether friends or foes, whether inside or outside. We are called to transcend the attitudes and the positions of others and relate to them at the *personal* level. The point is not how others relate to us, but how we relate to them as Christians. Even our enemies weep and rejoice; even our opposers get hungry and thirsty. If we can relate to them as persons and not as adversaries, there may be grounds for reconciliation—especially if we back off and let God do the judging. So, "if your enemy is hungry, feed him; if he is thirsty, give him drink; for by so doing you will heap burning coals upon his head" (12:20; cf. Prov. 25:21–22).

This does not mean that we are to make the hotheads more hotheaded! (The Bible says, "A soft answer turneth away wrath"— besides that, it makes them madder than anything else you can do! I don't think that's quite the idea, either.) The "coals" imagery goes back to an old Egyptian practice, representing the penitence of one who had a genuine change of heart. The idea is that a Christlike response to opposition may produce "burning shame" on the part of the opposer, and so bring about the conditions of reconciliation.

William Barclay says that the only way to really destroy an enemy is to make him a friend. I wish I would see more of this sort of "opposition transformation" or "enemy elimination" than I do.

● The Church and the World

Paul's treatment of church and state in 13:1–7 is so brief that one could almost assume that in his day the relationships between the two were simple and clear-cut. Not true. Early Christians lived under the political domination of Roman dictatorship, and their civil status was always threatened. By A.D. 49, Emperor Claudius had expelled the Jews, including Christian Jews, from Rome. By the time Romans was written (about A.D. 55), Nero was on the throne, and many Jews had returned. They were granted limited religious and civil freedom, but their situation was still insecure. Some Bible scholars think that Gentiles in the Roman congregation were in the mood to assert their political independence in Christ as well as their religious freedom.

All this helps us understand the words of Paul exhorting the Roman Christians to submit to governmental authority. One Jewish expulsion was enough; the church certainly did not need to be viewed as the source of political insurgency or anarchy. Paul is not teaching that the man on the throne of civil government is God's man and is therefore to be obeyed. But he believes God's providence includes the authority of the state. There is no anarchy in Paul. He declares that Christians are to be good citizens as far as possible, and they are to live in the state in good conscience.

I can write these words with little difficulty, for I live in peace and worship in peace. I have freedom to air my views and vote my conscience. Dietrich Bonhoeffer, reading the same Bible I read and following the same Christ I follow, was compelled to join a conspiracy to destroy the demonic power of Adolf Hitler. Martin Luther King, Jr., reading the same Bible I read and following the same Christ I follow, was compelled to join a peace march against the injustice of segregation. Bishop Desmond Tutu, reading the same Bible I read and following the same Christ I follow, has been constrained to take leadership in the struggle against South African apartheid. Other Christians are responding differently. None of these would deny the providential ordering of political government as such; nor would they deny the God-given responsibility to live under government as good citizens.

C. K. Barrett has compared our need of government with our need for sun and rain: Without them the world would not continue. They are the sources of life and goodness. They are also sometimes terrible in their destruction, and then we fight against them with all our might.

At times, Christians must resist bad government in the name of righteous government; they must resist bad law in the name of righteous law. In all cases, it seems to me, the *personal* issue must be one of conscience before God. Our problem is that heroic acts begun for the sake of righteousness often continue for the sake of ego. That is the fundamental issue to which both Paul and the Holy Spirit speak in Romans 13, regardless of our personal political situation or our personal political views.

● Our Obligation to Love

The theme of love in 13:8–14 ties this and the previous paragraph together. "Owe no one anything" seems to be the logical conclusion to the list of civic duties in 13:7. Society says: Pay your taxes, pay your respects—and you are paid up. Your obligations are fulfilled; you don't owe anybody anything. That is good law and good sense. But Paul's phrase, "except to love one another," confutes such worldly logic.

Jesus has brought a whole new perspective on the law, justice, and civil life. It is the way of love. It is defined, not by the world's system, but by his own self-giving. We are free in him to transcend the law ethic and live the life of love.

T. W. Manson suggests that there is no duty that is not included in "love," and there is nobody who is not included in "one another." Love is, then, the fulfilling of the law. Could it be that our civil-political problems are moral and spiritual, after all? Can we ever really believe love is the fulfilling of the law? Every great new plan to better our society is predicated on the assumption that there will be good will on all sides. Any reference to that "good will" is usually incidental. E. F. Scott reminds us that good will is, in fact, the one thing that really matters; and it is the one thing that the law can never produce.

I sense an urgency in this passage. We are to live in cooperation with the structures of this world, but they can never produce the dynamic for their own fulfillment. They are under judgment and will pass away with the soon coming of the Lord. We "know what hour it is" (13:11). All the more, then, we should live by power of Christ's love—love that has been "poured into our hearts through the Holy Spirit which has been given to us" (Rom. 5:5). In that love there is the fulfillment of whatever civil law demands; but more, in his love there is power to "cast off the works of darkness" and "put on the Lord Jesus Christ" (13:12, 14).

● Weak vs. Strong Members

Evidently, there was another kind of split developing in the fellowship of the Roman church. On one side were the "weak" (so called, I am sure, by the "strong"). They refrained from eating meat or drinking wine; they observed special religious days and regulations. So Paul's discussion here is a religious one. It has nothing to do with dieting for health or the modern alcohol problem. (A Christian's decision on whether or not to drink wine, for example, must be determined on other grounds than Paul's instructions here.) The "weak" believed they were on better terms with God than their "lax" brothers, and so they condemned them.

On the other side were the "strong" (so called, I am sure, by themselves), who were more relaxed, more "liberated" from such observances, and did not feel bound by any religious rules. They may have been like the Christians in Corinth who were saying, "All things are lawful" (1 Cor. 6:12; 10:23). They despised the stricter Christians. On the one side was a certain Pharisaism; on the other, a certain arrogance.

Barrett has made some helpful suggestions for interpreting this passage. For one thing, Barrett says we need to remember that the other Christian is a Christian; his identity as a Christian depends not on what I think, but on what Christ thinks of him. Paul does not compare those who are right and those who are wrong; he does not compare saints and sinners. He affirms that God has welcomed the other Christian, who may indeed be misguided in his opinions or wrong in his attitudes—but the Lord has welcomed him. I may need to discuss ethical and lifestyle issues with another believer, but I must not judge him.

For another thing, Barrett points out my brother—whether I call him strong or weak—has a conscience. If that conscience tells him to keep certain disciplines or not to keep them, I must not mock his conscience. If I do, I may hurt the individual, split the church, or influence the other person to do something that is really against conscience. If that person thus sins, then I sin because I have made him sin.

There seem to be two overarching principles in the passage: (1) Do not violate conscience—even if that conscience is not entirely enlightened. (2) Do not divide the fellowship. Never for the sake of such things should we destroy the unity of the body. We know from Paul's other writings that matters of faith cannot be negotiated. We are saved by faith, not by diet nor days nor law nor works. But in the body, faith is not enough; there must be love—love of the kind manifested in Jesus (15:1–6). Without love, the discipline of faith can become an exercise in judgment and destroy the body for which Christ died. The freedom of faith can become an exercise in rights and also destroy the body for which Christ died.

So we conclude our consideration of some of the great themes of Romans. The righteousness of God has been revealed in Christ to save us all—sinners without distinction. By his redemption we are brought into his body the church—Christians without distinction—enabled by his Spirit to live out our freedom in Christ.

● Discussion Questions

1. We have dealt with the question before, but it needs discussing one more time because we are never far from the problem: How do we keep the church's good advice or exhortations from becoming "rules"?

2. What are some things that make the good moral behavior of Christians different from the good moral behavior of others—or is there any real difference?

3. Are there any practical ways we can find out if we are thinking of ourselves more highly than we ought?

4. Discuss as realistically as you can some of the problems involved in having Jews and Gentiles in the same church (as in Acts 15). Could your church handle such problems? Could you? Discuss.

5. In the light of the Book of Romans, is there any place for ethnic churches?

6. Who do you think the enemy is in Romans 12:14–21? From the teaching of this paragraph, could the enemy ever be someone in the church of today? Discuss.

7. Do you agree with the way I have interpreted 13:1–7? Why did not the early church get involved in politics? Does that mean we should not? Discuss.

8. How do you respond to the illustrations of Bonhoeffer, King, and Bishop Tutu? Are they valid examples of Christian involvement? Discuss.

9. Discuss the statement "we are saved by faith; but in the body, faith is not enough."